The Snare of the Fowler

The Snare of the Fowler

Frankie Fonde Brogan

✓Chosen Books, Lincoln, Virginia 22078
of The Zondervan Corporation
Grand Rapids, Michigan 49506

THE SNARE OF THE FOWLER

Copyright © 1982 Frankie Fonde Brogan

Library of Congress Cataloging in Publication Data

Brogan, Frankie Fonde.
    The snare of the fowler.

1. Brogan, Frankie Fonde.   2. Episcopalians—United States—
Biography.   3. Brogan, Bob.   4. Children of God (Movement)   I. Title.
BX5995.B757A37   1982   248.2'46'0924 [B]   82-17740
ISBN 0-310-60280-7

Printed in the United States of America.

Chosen Books is a division of The Zondervan Corporation, Grand Rapids,
Michigan 49506. Editorial offices for Chosen Books are in Lincoln, Virginia
22078

To TOM,
my brave partner,
who has encouraged my pilgrimage,
not afraid to allow me
the delight of discovering
the uniqueness of
who I am.

Contents

Acknowledgments

This story was woven into the fabric of my life and I committed it to paper, but many contributed to the book. Some were
aware of their part and some were not. With grateful heart I
express my thanks to my friend Mary Lok, who unwittingly
spoke the right words at the right moment, setting me free to
embark on this adventure; to my family for lovingly giving me
the time and space I needed; to my husband, Tom, who acted
as sounding board, editor and honest critic, as well as wailing
wall, best friend and handholder; and to my remarkable
mother, nearly ninety, who has never wavered in her belief in
me and what I am about.

I also thank my friends and relatives, too numerous to
mention by name, who read the manuscript and offered
tough constructive criticism as well as affirmation; the many
people who gave me permission to include them in these
pages; friends who lent a hand with the typing—Jeff Cothran,
Lynne Moody, Pam Wolf, Barbara Colby, and especially Patty
Turney, who under great pressure miraculously put the whole
second draft onto a word processor in a month; E. K. (Charlie)
Salls who gave of his time and expertise to proofread the
original manuscript, and whose editorial advice, perceptive
comments and objective viewpoint were greatly needed;
Madeleine L'Engle, whose *Crosswicks Journals* inspired me to

persist and who sent me in a letter "a large dose of stubbornness"; and Ruth Vaughn, author of *Write to Discover Yourself*, whose faith in my writing gave me confidence to persevere.

I close with thankful appreciation to the entire staff of Chosen Books, whose patience with this neophyte has known no bounds. Special thanks to my editor, Leonard LeSourd, whose professional yet gentle editorial skills have taught me much. Accolades to his secretary, the incredible Alice Watkins, who with cheerful patience walked and talked me through the many new and unexpected twists and turns in the publishing road. And finally, my deep thanks to the gracious Catherine Marshall for blessing me with such a warm welcome to a new world.

Introduction

When I began reading *The Snare of the Fowler,* all I knew about Frankie Brogan was that this was her first book. I was unprepared for the golden reading experience that followed.

Frankie Brogan writes passionately, poignantly and movingly about what is close to her—her family. *The Snare of the Fowler* describes a painful experience, the abrupt leaving home of her son to join a religious cult. Nothing new about this—thousands of families have gone through and are going through this kind of trauma. Many of their children never return home. Some return embittered, rebellious, alienated. A few come home and find healing and a new life.

At the beginning Frankie was resentful toward her stubborn, brainwashed son and angry with God. But she did not flee the situation, enshrouded in self-pity. Instead, she sought help from a God she did not really know but dared to trust. It began a whole new life for her.

I'll not give away the ending of this beautifully told story, except to say that the suspenseful Brogan family adventure so thrilled me that I could scarcely wait to meet them and hear their experiences firsthand.

Every mother and father who is concerned about the world's influence on their children ought to read this book. It shows how a parent can turn to God with a seemingly hopeless situation and be joyfully surprised by the practical solution He gives.

I salute Frankie Brogan for her sensitive writing skills, her honesty, and willingness to be vulnerable. The depth of her spiritual perceptions could have come only because she was willing to walk with the Lord down a lonely, rock-strewn path. The result for the reader is riches.

Catherine Marshall
Boynton Beach, Florida

1

A Corner Turned

On Sunday, March 21, 1971, my husband and I came in refreshed from an afternoon outing and saw a note on the kitchen counter.

Have you ever noticed how it is possible to turn a corner in your life and not even realize that the scene has changed—at least, not at first?

I picked up the note and examined it. It was scrawled in a bold hand in bright red letters made with a wide magic marker. The ink had spread out on the porous scratchpad paper, but it was still legible:

> *Mom and Dad,*
> *I met some people in the park today called the Children of God and I'm going to visit with them a couple of days in Brenham. Just tell the store I'm sorry but this is more important.*
> *I love you.*
> *Praise God!*
>
> > *Bob*

In small handwriting with a regular ballpoint pen was an afterthought—a phone number to be used in case of emergency. That was all. There was a sense of finality about it.

1

I handed it to Tom with question marks showing in my eyes. He read it over silently, said, "Hmm . . ." a few times, and nothing more.

"What do you think it means?" I queried, pressing.

He read it again, then said, "Just what it says, I suppose. Don't overreact, Frankie." And he hugged me.

Since I do tend to overreact, and I knew Tom loved me and helped me keep things in proportion, I tried to push down the bubbles of unrest that were threatening to surface. Tom settled down with some reading in his favorite chair in the den adjoining the kitchen, while I read the note again.

The paper was uneven at the bottom, as if something had been torn off. Call it a mother's intuition; call it my detective instinct (I love mystery books!); call it just plain nosiness, if you like. But I opened the door to the closet where the trash was, and saw immediately the wad of paper with the telltale red ink winking up at me. It was right on top. My unsuspecting son hadn't even tried to bury it from his mother's prying eyes.

I spread it out carefully, smoothing out the wrinkles, and read:

Mom and Dad,
Sue and Kathy,
Don't freak out but I have gone to live with . . .

No more. He had torn it off, started again with less ominous-sounding phraseology, and left us his second effort.

I'm afraid I did "freak out," but quietly and slowly. I held it back from my placidly reading husband for a few moments, while the past few years bounced through my head like ping-pong balls.

What now? What now?

I glanced around at the warm comfort of our home. Since the Depression days of my youth, I'd longed and worked toward just this kind of ease and affluence. Here in Houston, Texas, we'd found our dream at last. Located in a fine neighborhood, with lovely neighbors, excellent schools and our Episcopal church only blocks away, what could have gone wrong?

In my mind's eye, I saw our children meeting the challenges that all youth of these times have had to face in a kaleidoscope world of change—long hair, miniskirts, hard rock, drugs and alcohol, relaxed morals, teenage marriages and pregnancies and abortions—et cetera, et cetera.

Our oldest child, Becki, was now safely and happily married, with one daughter, living in Detroit. Susan, our second daughter, was due to graduate from Trinity University in San Antonio in May, and was engaged to be married. Kathy, our baby, was attending St. Stephen's, an Episcopal boarding school in Austin. She was home for spring break at the moment.

And Bob, our only son, the second of four children, a child of promise—handsome, bright and gifted with scholastic and athletic prowess as well as lyrical musical ability—had been one of those affected by the changing world scene. He had had his share of conflicts, had handled some well and some not so well, but through it all had been loved and supported by us.

I pictured them as jugglers, all juggling the same wild psychedelic balls of the new age. The girls had become expert. But Bob simply couldn't juggle. Some months back, everything in his life had suddenly crescendoed into a loud and final discordant note, as all he was trying to handle had crashed around him at once.

Then a dramatic change had occurred. He told us he'd "met

Jesus Christ"; that peace had come to him. He seemed to be refocused. We didn't understand it, but we knew something important had happened—perhaps a crisis conversion. The reality of it affected those around him. His joy was honest and awesome. Whether from God or not, it was cause for rejoicing, and we did not question it much.

With a mother's eye, I saw him as recovering from a kind of sickness. Now at age 23, the lost years behind him, he wanted to get the education he had abandoned. His depression from a failed youthful marriage seemed to be over. As a college dropout, however, he would have to do some backtracking. The temporary job he held at a local store was boring, but part of the necessary regrouping plan.

Yet I could see new purpose in him. He even spoke of becoming a minister. I envisioned the Episcopal seminary at Sewanee, but dropped it when I saw he leaned toward a Bible college. I felt I was becoming more pliable through the trials we'd gone through with him.

As the details of all this past chaotic turmoil whirled around in living color in my mind, the panic bubbles began to surface. I ran to Tom for support and comfort.

"Honey, look at this! He wrote what he *really* meant in this first note. This is wrong—I know it! Who are these Children of God, anyway?" A rush of words colored with fear poured out of me.

"Don't overreact," Tom said again as he studied the note. "Let's give him a chance. He's been so reasonable lately. He'll know himself if it's not right—give him a chance. Anyway, there'll be plenty of time for us to look into it with him."

Tom would discuss it no more. We looked at each other bleakly. I knew him too well. He was worried, too.

We had turned a corner, just like that.

2

The "Forsaking"

We didn't hear anything from Bob until Tuesday. That afternoon, a large van covered with Christian symbols and slogans drew up in front of our house.

Through the years with Bob's music combos—"The Glass Kans" and "Michael"—I thought I had become inured to weird vehicles and strangely garbed kids. The equipment trailer of the "Glass Kans" had been dented in on top and someone had painted a giant footprint there the full length of the vehicle. It was visible only from the second story of our house, but it had always made me smile. I felt a lump in my throat now, remembering it. That stage had seemed so simple and uncomplicated—a phase he was going through. Grin and bear it. It will pass.

But this new group . . . . Why did I have such a wrong presentiment about it? A liberal Episcopalian should not mind when Christianity is being expressed in ways other than the old, comfortable ones. I had never even heard of the Children of God. Why did that sound so threatening to me? And if there were apron strings left, I needed to cut them, and I knew it.

I gathered my thoughts and concluded that I was being

5

ridiculously unfair. I needed to give the thing a chance, as Tom had said, instead of making a snap judgment.

I'll be a loving observer, I decided, *and keep my hands out of it.* My mouth closed. Tom was away on business that day, and the whole thing rested in my lap.

My private vow was put to a hard test, for these four or five boys, along with Bob, had come to take with them all of Bob's worldly possessions.

Bob came in looking happy—yet anxious, too. He seemed subtly different in some way I couldn't pin down. I knew he wanted me to accept him and his belief in what he was doing. I had always had good rapport with the friends he brought home, and knew he wanted me to treat these young men the same way. It seemed important that I try.

All of them except Bob looked slightly seedy, like the poor souls I'd heard unkindly called "poor white trash" when I was growing up in Tennessee. Their shabbiness lacked the elan of the modern teenager in his patched jeans and frayed T-shirt. Also, a faint servility in their manner simply didn't ring true to me. It grated on my already-tense nerves.

They all swept through the house, emptying it swiftly of any reminder of my son: his clothes, books, bike, tape recorder, and musical equipment, including a guitar, sax and banjo. And I didn't lift a finger, just stood there smiling and trying to act natural, keeping a tight rein on my emotions. I did tell them politely that the bedroom furniture in his room was ours, not Bob's; and then I felt unaccountably ashamed when they nodded agreeably and left it sitting there.

I learned that they were all to "forsake" worldly possessions. Another thing each forsook was his name. Each "Child of God" took on a biblical name and went solely by that name from then on. Bob's new name had not yet been selected, but the thought of this abandonment of identity shook me more than seeing all of my son's material things vanishing into the van.

Kathy popped in, all eyes and ears. Bob, who adored his 16-year-old sister and was always tender with her, introduced her to the "Children" and let her help them move things out to the sidewalk.

The whole episode still has a faded sense of unreality about it for me. The numbness that developed when I held my emotions in such tight check may have fogged my recollection. In any case, most of my memory of that day is hazy.

A couple of incidents, however, stand out as if a bright spotlight were trained on them. The first one came when I wandered into the living room and glanced outside to see Kathy kneeling without embarrassment right on the sidewalk in front of the house—her hands in the air, her face aglow, repeating some words I couldn't hear given her by an attractive young man with dark curly hair.

I was stabbed with the poignant remembrance of my favorite beach ball floating silently, relentlessly out with the tide when I was only three and we were visiting Grandmother in Florida. The same aching emptiness embraced me now. Were all my children slipping away out of reach?

Later I remember feeding the whole bunch, Jewish mother fashion, trying to keep them long enough for Tom to show up and somehow miraculously reverse the whole procedure, like a movie film running backwards. I couldn't begin to recall the exact conversation around the table, except that it was laced with *Alleluias*, *Praise the Lords* and Scripture quotations that were, to me, unfamiliar.

The other sharply focused moment came when, quite innocently, I asked Bob when he would be back or when we could come to see him. There followed a chilling silence, as if time had stopped; and I realized I had stepped into forbidden territory.

One young man called Stephen, who had rubbed me the wrong way from the first with his self-righteous air and bully-boy manner, flashed Bob a hard order with his eyes. It was an unspoken command to *Set things straight with your mother, you punk.* But I caught it.

I was certain Bob would not take it from someone like this pipsqueak, so much younger and obviously less endowed with intelligence and the simple graces. But I was left speech-less when Bob explained to me humbly that he was only a "babe" and had no say over such things.

They left quickly with the curt announcement that someone would be by to pick up Bob's car later in the week.

When they had gone, I hoped that "bad dream" aura would go, too. But it clung, forcing me to face the reality of what was happening.

Tom came home and was incredulous when I stumbled through my description of the afternoon. Kathy had a dazed, glowing look on her face. She explained to us shyly that she had accepted Jesus and wanted to visit Bob at Zion, the name of the colony in Brenham, near Houston.

We tried to relate warmly to this news, but our thoughts and emotions were with our son. I went to bed with a headache, berating myself for what I *should* have said and done, and didn't; and wondering if it would have made any difference anyhow.

3

My Dream Family

In my adult life, whenever I need courage or faith or peace, my thoughts flee to the hills of my childhood. Reaching out to the warm contentment that was mine, I find myself humming songs that were sung around a campfire long ago at a Girl Scout camp tucked away in the heart of the Smoky Mountains.

The summers I spent there cut through to an inner core of my being and left an indelible imprint. We camped without electricity in primitive splendor in real tents, and slept on straw mattresses we had stuffed ourselves. We sang songs about the river, the mountains and "Great Spirit," Indian fashion. We were exposed to important things: Me, You, Nature and God.

The oldest of five children born to Charles and Rhea Fonde, I grew up near the foothills of the Smokies in Knoxville, Tennessee, in a quiet neighborhood on the eastern edge of town called, appropriately, Morningside. We could see the Smoky Mountains clearly from our back porch. That distant purple mountain range, crowned with a misty haze, rims the consciousness of my mind. Just how deeply I was influenced

9

by the serenity and majesty of those hills, I'm only beginning to realize.

But all was not beauty and wonder and light in the Depression years. With so many mouths to feed, and with a father more interested in sports and nature than in the business world, it is no wonder I used to hear them talk about "the wolf at the door." It would be late at night when I should have been asleep, but was huddled instead in secret misery at the top of the stairs, hearing them talk and picturing a real wolf outside ready to pounce.

Our family attended St. John's Episcopal Church in downtown Knoxville. My earliest recollections of it include a fierce elderly man who used to loom large in the pulpit high above me, pounding on it with vigor, as his voice thundered and boomed around his silent congregation. God seemed awfully stern.

This loudness is balanced in my memory, however, by soft-voiced Sunday school teachers who loved two mysterious books—the Bible and the prayer book. These people spoke of a God of love.

When I close my eyes now and think back to those days, I remember our modest little house set on the slope of a hill with weeping mulberry bushes in front; flower gardens and a grape arbor on the sides; and a chicken house, swingset, sandpile and (later) a badminton court in back.

Though our furniture was shabby and the carpets worn, and though our fights were loud and the rivalry fierce, it was a place where love and acceptance ruled. Whenever I dream of *home*, even today, I dream of that place and those folks. I had an unusually happy home life.

And in times of stress, my mind reaches deep into those inner recesses of who I am, searching for that sense of security, that remembrance of being carefully nurtured, that forms the essence of me.

A clear picture of my mother emerges. Standing on the side porch, wiping her hands on her apron, she calls in her rich Southern voice, "Henry, Anne, Alice, Rhea—I mean, Frankie!"

As generations of mothers have done, my mother would tick off the names of all her children before getting to the one she wanted. I couldn't understand it then, but have smiled at myself as I have done the same when calling my own.

Again, a little louder: "Frankie! Fah-ran-kee, where are you-u-u? Time for lunch!"

Where am I, indeed? Here I am, Mama, under the weeping mulberry bush, hidden away in my secret place, listening to the sounds of my world, absorbing the sights through leafy boughs that flow to the ground and spread out on the grass like a bride's train. It's so safe here, Mama—so quiet and cool and shadowy on a summer's day.

I hear Caroline's mother calling her, too. She's my close friend who lives next door; and because she's an only child, her mother has no long list of names to shout, poor thing. Caroline is a brilliant, witty, beautiful child, to whom everything comes easily. She has no idea how seriously she challenges me. She has become my yardstick, and what she accomplishes with no apparent effort I am determined to do also, but it takes dogged determination and hard work.

Now I hear Daddy's car stop, and I watch him, his red hair shining in the sun, bounding across the front yard and entering the house. Former captain of the University of Tennessee football team, he moves with the grace of a natural athlete down memory's corridors. Bright blue eyes twinkling with evident good humor, he's a strong, firm, highly principled man's man.

Now that he's home, I hasten to answer Mother's call, darting out of my sanctuary while no one is watching, knowing that my father expects each of us to be seated at table, fresh and fully dressed, at every meal.

At lunch I find my three blonde, curly haired sisters seated with my brother, whose straight brown hair matches mine. It seems to me, being the plain firstborn with Henry second, that my parents improved their creative abilities somehow, turning out prettier and prettier models as the years unfolded.

It isn't fair!

Mother, detecting a budding inferiority complex in her eldest, often cupped my face in her hands and, looking deep into my eyes, would say I had personality when I felt like a lump. She would convince me I could win when I felt like a loser. A great beauty herself, with dark, lustrous hair and enormous, expressive eyes, she was very persuasive.

On this day she asks me about our morning activities, but I'm evasive. How can I tell them of my spot under the mulberry bush and the dreams that grow there? No one would understand my fantasy world peopled with my shadowy future family.

There's a handsome husband who cherishes me, and a number of children; but everything, strangely, seems to revolve around the son who will one day be mine. He's a little boy with dark hair and blue eyes—smart, bright, agile, a born leader with winning ways. The others are indistinct, but I can see him plainly. It's as if I've always known him.

I have never heard of anyone else whose childish musings focused so much on one future son.

In high school years, I began to look for the man who would father my dream son. Since I had a mental image of this child, in both character and appearance, I searched for someone with similar qualities. Meanwhile, I won honors and made a name for myself. In fact, I developed into a successful people-pleaser, feeling like the queen of my world.

I entered the University of Tennessee intent on enlarging my realm and looking seriously for the one who would share my throne.

Then, at a summer school dance under the east basket of the basketball court—"my" spot on the dance floor—with the big band sound swirling around me, Tom Brogan came into view. He'd come to Knoxville to complete his pilot training. There he stood, as someone introduced us, the smiling grownup edition of my secret son! Though he embodied the son, he was real, and at once became more important than the dream.

It was a moment of recognition. Tom had been conducting a search of his own, and I fitted his picture amazingly. He had graduated from the University of Richmond at the ripe age of 19, with a Phi Beta Kappa key to his credit. Because of his youth while in college, he never felt quite accepted by his peers, and longed for a "Betty Coed" to fall for him, so that he in turn would be one of the gang. To him, I was that "girl of his dreams."

Thus, for flighty, unsubstantial reasons, two people were drawn together with marriage in mind.

Yet somehow we had been prepared uniquely for each other. Our backgrounds were similar. His family had four boys and one girl. Our parents emphasized the same ethical values. And, although my family had stayed put and his had moved a lot, he had lived in neighborhoods with a Morningside atmosphere. In college he had left his family's church (Roman Catholic), but contented me by saying that he was now willing to consider becoming an Episcopalian.

During our teens, we had both been affected by what I've come to call the "Andy Hardy Days of Innocence." The Andy

Hardy movie series, featuring Mickey Rooney and Judy Garland, was intended only as light entertainment. Yet somehow it was adopted by many of our peers as a model of the way life is.

Set in a neighborhood not unlike Morningside, it depicted life as simple and straightforward, with no hint of crime or drugs or any such unpleasantness. Andy's first kiss required months of public preparation to lessen the shock. Subconsciously we identified with that life, because we were part of a similar scene that we expected would go on forever.

The Andy Hardy days, however, were not a good ideal. Their innocence was naive. Their serenity was superficial. Their happiness was shallow. They masked much, and were simply not real.

We were to discover this the hard way. Our generation was .totally unprepared for the one that was coming.

4

My Dream Family Becomes Real

Pearl Harbor, followed by the Second World War, shocked us. But we weathered that trauma. And in the postwar days, we did our best to hang on to the Andy Hardy concept.

Tom and I married in January 1944. Tom was stationed as a pilot in San Francisco when our first child, Rebecca Anne, was born. Becki grew up to be a darling redhead, with the strong, dominant character associated with the firstborn child. She was beyond my comprehension and certainly out of my control much of the time.

About two-and-a-half years later, the war over and Tom flying for an airline out of New York, my dream son was born—Robert Thomas Brogan, Jr. Though a homely baby, as the months passed Bob began to resemble what I'd longed for in my son.

Then came an unexpected surprise: another baby was on the way. As if to let me know it was not to his liking, Bob stopped sleeping. Pacing the floor with him became a nightly ritual.

One night I had a fleeting impulse to open the window of our fifth-floor apartment and sail with the child of my dreams, as well as the unplanned one, to oblivion. It was an alluring thought that grew more compelling as the evenings continued to string out one after the other with no seeming end.

With strength from some unknown source, I was able to hold back these dark thoughts, keeping them from turning into action. Although physical exhaustion precipitated them, I dimly recognized that more was wrong with my world than lack of sleep. I didn't discuss it with Tom. I couldn't even admit it to myself.

Then, slowly, like one of those crystal ball snow scenes, my world began to right itself, and the snow stopped whirling. Bob began to sleep again. Susan, a blonde child of quietness and patience, was born—and seemed to say in her silence, "I don't want to cause any trouble." My world came back into focus and peace descended upon us.

We were living in New York City when our first major crisis occurred. Becki and Susan woke up with polio on the same day and were rushed to the hospital. Everything possible was soon being done.

Well, almost. We had had our children christened, but had not been attending church. Without discussing it, Tom and I both felt the need for the added insurance of asking for God's help. Tom slipped over to a nearby Catholic church to pray. And I talked to the Episcopal priest on the phone, and then to God right through the window, asking Him to spare Bob and heal the girls.

Bob did not contract polio, and though the two girls had to have therapy sessions for a year, they recovered with no visible crippling effects. This episode rocked us enough, however, that we decided we needed to pay our "dues," or make our insurance payments to God. Tom took confirmation classes and eventually became an Episcopalian. And by this time, living out on Long Island, we joined an Episcopal church near us.

Katherine King Brogan, our third daughter, put in her appearance six years after Susan's birth, and we had another redhead. I used to say, "If I could just 'do' Becki again, I don't think I'd make as many mistakes." When I saw Kathy for the first time, it flashed through my mind that God had heard me and was giving me a second chance. I was flooded with love for her and for Him, and felt *I* could do it this time.

Our next jolt came when Kathy was a year old and the doctors discovered she had a congenital hip dislocation. She had to be put into a complete body cast from chest to toetips. When our Episcopal priest suggested a healing service, I agreed, though I'd never heard of such a thing.

Again, as before, there was a ràpid recovery—so rapid that our Catholic doctor referred to it in hushed tones as a miracle. I wanted to believe it, but soon found natural explanations for her recovery.

Tom had started out after the war with an airline, but entered the business world reluctantly after Bob's birth. He did well in business, and eventually ended up in an executive position with a large advertising agency, where he is today.

Tom's life in the business world kept him away a lot, and I easily took up the reins he put down. I ran things at home; it seemed natural, expedient, necessary. When he came home he wanted peace and quiet, or fun and jollies. And I tried to provide what he wanted. The children were my province, and I managed them, our home and my multifaceted community responsibilities as well as I could.

I gave Tom the full financial responsibility, but subtly ran the show myself. Secretly I loved being in charge. After all, I'd been doing it for years, even before marriage, and I was good at it. My father used to chant teasingly, to the tune of *Whatever Lola Wants:* "Whatever Frankie wants, Frankie gets." I felt proud of my ability to handle a three-ring circus.

By 1958 Tom had been transferred from New York to Detroit, and we had a pleasant home on the grounds of an old orchard in Bloomfield Hills. There we became the familiar picture of the typical American suburban household in the '50s. Only occasionally were we staggered by a shocking happening, such as when one of Bob's good friends drowned learning to scuba-dive, or when a friend who seemed on top of things suddenly shot himself. Nothing was supposed to go wrong in our Andy Hardy world.

Our children were growing up. Kathy, about four when we first arrived in Bloomfield Hills, was my entrance to neighborhood coffees. Everyone came to know this natural child who projected love and joy, and was eager to meet her mom. I basked in the reflected glory, and delighted in being known as "Kathy's mom." And she did not limp! *She did not limp.*

Our quiet one, Susan, grew tall and lanky and became our loud one. She loved horses and rode beautifully on a drill team, English style. When Bob taught her to play the guitar, they became quite a folk duo, entertaining us and friends.

Becki began to channel her determined willfulness into scholarly pursuits and became a top student. She went to Spain on an exchange program, lived with a Spanish family, attended some classes at the University of Madrid, and arrived home thinking in Spanish.

Then there was Bob, endowed with much natural ability. We were touched by his budding musical gifts: singing unexpected solos in school and at church functions; and writing words and music of his own. He learned a chord system on the piano and taught himself to play the guitar. And his natural athletic prowess led him to leadership roles in sports—catcher in baseball, quarterback in football. My dream child was fleshing out.

But when Becki entered college and elected to go her own way by embracing current mores that were foreign to us, I couldn't take it. One of my "subjects" was seriously misbehaving.

And there was more than that wrong with my world. Other things were slipping out of my grasp, too. Once again I fell into a deep depression, this time requiring professional assistance. Dimly I realized that my help could come only from God, from the faith I had breathed in as a child, from the faith I knew was real, if buried.

My psychiatrist tried to steer me away from such delusion, but one day I crawled into our church office with some of my dark poems in hand. An associate rector took me in and let me share my pain with him. I remember reading him one poem about a loathsome pit that described the dark, ugly place I found myself.

There was a long silence. His eyes gazed at me with deep compassion. Then he spoke softly. His words were words of life:

"Oh, Frankie, don't you know there is One who will go into that pit with you? He is with you now. He's the only One who can bring you out. And He will. He is faithful."

I slept without tranquilizers that night and the next. My recovery began from that moment. That priest's faith acted as a transfusion for my own anemic faith. But characteristically, when praised by my psychiatrist at our last session as having accomplished much of the recovery myself, I accepted his evaluation. I walked out of his office once more in control of my life, my head high.

Although I didn't really give any credit to anything outside myself, something had happened during this experience that stayed with me, and sustained me when I saw our son faltering and his world spinning out of control. It hurt, and I ached, but I didn't fall apart as before. Some foundation had been laid that acted as a net does for a trapeze artist. I knew the pit was there, but I also knew there was a safety device to catch me from the awful plunge. And I felt I could depend on it.

It felt good to have the security of that net as we embarked on a new chapter of our lives. Tom was moved from an automotive to an oil account, and that meant Houston instead of Detroit.

Although change creates stress for us humans, I was beginning to learn that without change there can be no growth.

5

Texas Storm

Our move to Texas in 1965 was destined to have a profound and far-reaching effect on our family. It began when I was gripped by a powerful paralysis of indecision after several heady househunting days in the infant metropolis of Houston.

Tom, catching me stifling tears of frustration, made an uncharacteristic suggestion.

"Frankie," he asked tentatively, "why don't we pray about all this?"

I was surprised into silence. We knelt beside the hotel bed together, and he talked to God in a conversational way, asking for guidance in our home selection and for His blessing on our move.

I couldn't remember our doing such a thing since the girls had had polio. In fact, I wasn't even sure we had done it together then. I became embarrassed, and after a while tried to take hold of the situation by interrupting with, "That's enough, that's enough."

Yet the effect of the prayer was instant calm. We seemed to

have suddenly entered the eye of the storm. By noon we had found our home, and it was perfect for us.

Though the girls had complained the loudest about this move, they made the quickest adjustment. Bob went around bolstering everyone else's morale while he silently withered away inside. It was his senior year in high school. He had carved a niche for himself in Michigan—first-string quarterback, class leader, top parts in school plays—but he found that this niche couldn't be transplanted instantly to Texas, especially since he was cut out of his favorite sport, football, by a state rule.

It was a pivotal time in our son's life, and we didn't like the changes we began to see in him. Recognizing that his search for identity was in full gear, however, we tried not to overreact to things we did not understand, as long as they seemed relatively minor in the larger picture.

Beatlemania was in full swing, and Bob and his newly formed rock group, the "Glass Kans," were pioneers among their peers in things like long hair and new dress fads. The "Glass Kans" were in demand, and even cut a record that was played on the local radio station. On the surface it appeared that Bob, and indeed our whole family, had made a smooth transition.

Though Bob had been active in our church through the years, now he scorned it and our faith. We'd been involved in altar guild, choir, vestry, and men's and women's groups, but Bob held up a mirror to us, in effect, and said, "Look at yourselves. You're not living the life described in the Bible. In fact, I've never seen anyone who did."

We were involved in what Bob called "churchianity." It made me angry and defensive, partly because I sensed some truth in his words.

Bob's main focus soon became his combo with its rock

music. It was so important to him that he based his college choice on his desire to keep the band together.

Tom and I argued about this. I believed that a smaller college would be better for Bob. I sensed that his motives were wrong, and that his emphasis on a rock group would lead to trouble.

Tom agreed with me in principle, but felt we should not force another move upon Bob on the heels of the transfer from Michigan. He could see merit in Bob's plan, and felt we should show confidence in our son by allowing him to make the decision.

So Bob entered the University of Houston.

At first it seemed to go well. But by Bob's sophomore year, with the combo living together in a rented house, his grades began to suffer. Bob vowed to settle down and study harder. He was not used to failure. We believed in him, knew his potential, and tried to disregard a growing uneasiness.

Besides, I loved the guys in the combo; they had become part of our lives. I thought of them, naively, as little boys. That they could represent powerful attractions to the opposite sex or that they might dabble in drugs never crossed my mind. Drugs to us were something dispensed by the local pharmacist in exchange for a prescription.

Fortunately, with perhaps one exception, none of these boys became involved seriously in the drug scene, although they were involved. Girls were drawn to them like magnets and made themselves at home at their rented "pad." We appeared on the premises only when invited, like good Andy Hardy parents. And on these few occasions, of course, all was in order.

Yet none of this fit the pattern of our expectations for our son.

In the beginning we felt out-of-sync, as if the rhythm of our life had gotten off-kilter. We tried to change step to catch the new cadence. But there was always a different beat. The faint rustlings of danger in the distance moved inexorably closer, increasing in volume, until the force of a whirlwind was upon us and we recognized it for what it was. By then, we were powerless to do anything but hold on and observe the destruction.

It reminded me of when Tom and I had been stationed in Missouri during the war, and I was shopping in St. Joseph alone one afternoon.

Almost without warning, a strange yellow cast enveloped the town, creating instant unease in me. People began to run, panic on their faces, and no one would stop to answer my anxious questions. I could hear a strange sound getting louder and closer. Suddenly, as the sound crescendoed in power, a nearby plate-glass window popped out and lay in shattered slivers on the pavement. Then, as quickly as it had begun, the sound began to diminish into the distance. Premature darkness soaked up the yellow sky like a sponge, and I took hurried shelter from a heavy deluge.

Eventually I learned that we had been on the edge of a small tornado—a "twister." No one was seriously hurt, and damage was slight, but I never forgot my sense of bewildered helplessness during those brief minutes. The memory of that little scene haunted me like a bad dream, and made it feel like *déjà vu*, as we watched our son caught up in spiraling circumstances beyond his or our control.

It also seemed to me that Bob's life lay in fragments around him, like the plate-glass window back in Missouri. He failed in an early marriage, quit school, then started and quit again. He tried to find himself in his music and in many other ways, brushed aside our efforts to help, and struggled on his own, doggedly determined to make order out of chaos. But the jigsaw of his life would not fit together. He was ashamed to come to us for help. Despair seemed to get a stranglehold on him.

Then one afternoon, while Tom was at work, Bob walked in with a spring in his step and a new light in his eyes. There was a softness and sweetness about him that brought a catch to my throat. I knew instantly that this new gentleness reflected an inner strength and purpose.

I sensed excitement in him as he began to open up in an honest, revealing way, more deeply than he had since childhood. My heart skipped a beat as he began. Perhaps he would be ready to come back home and start life anew!

Bob told me that one day in his "pad," he had noticed a New English Bible he had received at confirmation. He started browsing through it out of curiosity and a halfhearted desire to improve his mind. Romans, where he decided to begin, was a struggle. It made no sense to him at all. But, sticking to it stubbornly—he wasn't sure just why—he began to find himself strangely touched by the words he read there. Daily he read more. Meaningful messages leaped out at him, too often to be coincidental.

One day, swamped by his problems, alone in his room, he had flung himself on the floor full-length, with the Bible in his hand, and groaned: "God, if there is a God, help me! Get me out of this mess."

It was a pure and simple cry for help. He told me he had not really expected any change in his situation.

Then there came a phone call about a job. As Bob heard the voice on the line, offering him a ray of light, it seemed as though his other ear was filled with knowledge of One who was conveying the message: *I Am . . . . I am He who does this.*

And Bob described to me the amazing chain of events that

had started the very next day. First, at a hospital where he had gone to be with a friend, he met a young crewcut Baptist minister who talked and prayed with him.

Then, on the very day Bob was talking to me, he had gone to this young man's church.

"It was just a little frame building on stilts out in the middle of a field," he marveled. "It held only a few people. I sat in the back row. At the end of the service, the preacher said that anyone who had given his life to the Lord that week should come forward. And Mom, I felt he was speaking to me. I had in me this new knowledge of a loving force that was real. But my heart was beating so hard I couldn't move. Then the preacher said there was one who needed to come up front—a person who needed to make a public declaration of his new faith by coming forward."

A manipulative tactic used in altar calls, I thought as Bob talked. I had always harbored a secret scorn for people who responded to altar calls, considering that to be ostentation of the worst sort.

"The man sitting next to me leaned over and offered to walk up with me," Bob continued. "I don't know how he knew I was the one. I wondered if my heart was beating so loud he could hear it! Anyhow, I told the man I'd go by myself—and I did. I went up to the altar. I was the only one who did."

Bob had a stunned stillness about him. True gladness lighted his face for the first time in months. Then his simmering excitement broke through with these words:

"Mother, it's true! He's real! I really did mean it when I went up front today. I have an absolute knowledge of the reality of Jesus. And Mom, He loves me, as awful as I am. He loves me!"

My eyes brimmed with tears. I was not sure I knew the same Reality. But those words touched me.

After Bob's conversion, the forecast was for balmy temperatures and fair skies. But the abrupt entrance of the Children of God into Bob's life several months later was like hearing the weatherman describe a tropical disturbance in the Caribbean heading our way.

Since we had already experienced one devastating hurricane, even the suspicion of another one, however remote, sent our caution flags flying.

6

A Visit to the Children of God

On Wednesday morning, the day after the "forsaking" episode in which Bob had come with his new comrades to clear out his personal belongings, I awoke with uneasy feelings.

I could still see Bob's things being carried outside and into the weirdly marked van parked out front. The face of the boy called Stephen kept bobbing through my thoughts and it had a smug, unwavering leer plastered on it. I felt my irritation rising.

So I decided to phone a woman who worked out of the same real estate office I did. She had shown much concern for Bob in his new walk of faith.

Frances Ryan was a "born-again" believer like Bob. When she had told me her story one day, for some reason I had not recoiled as I would have months before. Instead, I had told her about Bob's conversion, feeling she would understand his experience better than Tom or I did.

She had understood. She had also come to see him, and soon Bob began attending her church in another part of town.

The dismay in Frances' voice now as I described the turn of events sent my heart sinking. Then, when she offered to call

28

one of the elders in her church to obtain more information about the Children of God, my hopes began to rise. A roller-coaster ride had begun. Later the elder—a man named Newman B. Peyton, Jr.—called me to say he was doing some checking, but had been unable so far to discover anything about this group. He sounded baffled. I went sliding down again.

The next evening, with Tom home, Bob suddenly walked into the house looking perfectly normal and very happy. There were some boys and girls with him—new faces to me except for the boy who had led Kathy to pray in front of the house. I was relieved to see no sign of Stephen. They had come to tow Bob's ailing car to Brenham.

There was a difference in the whole scene this time, and I began to feel foolish. These young people seemed liked typical exuberant kids. Bob looked better than he had in ages, relaxed and full of joy. He assured Tom that this group was just what he needed.

"They've got purpose," he told us. "They're more dedicated than any church I've ever seen, and I'm finding real fulfillment for the first time in my life."

He was thoroughly convincing. Kathy, for her part, was fairly dancing with excitement.

We shared an enjoyable supper together, and afterward I found myself going through the cupboards and refrigerator, sacking everything I could spare for them to take back. I really wanted to help them.

Why had I been so reluctant? I could tell that Tom was accepting the situation with apparent ease. I caught him looking at me from time to time with a puzzled expression that said, "How on earth did you see so much to worry about? You and your imagination!"

While I was in the kitchen still packing food for the young people, I could see Tom and Bob in the den in private talk. They looked so "together."

Bob was convincing Tom, and later Tom persuaded me, that it would be all right for Kathy to go back to Brenham for a day or so to visit. Bob described the place they were staying at as a mansion. The girls' dorm was in the main building, while the boys lived in what had been a barn on the estate.

"You know how I love her, Dad," Bob said. "I wouldn't let anything happen to hurt her. This will be so good for her."

And so it was arranged. This was Thursday. Kathy wasn't due to return to school at St. Stephen's until Monday. We could go pick her up in Brenham on Saturday and have a chance to see it all for ourselves.

As we talked, I began to experience a return of the nagging uneasiness I'd known since reading the note on Sunday. But I was ashamed to admit it. Tom and Bob looked confident. Kathy was packing some things and chattering happily with her new friends. And I liked the girls. They seemed sensible and wholesome.

After they left, our home was suddenly silent and empty. Some magic had gone out of the moment. But I could see Tom was not feeling the letdown I was, and any discussion about it seemed unwise.

And anyway, how could I tell him that I was being reminded eerily of a childhood fairy tale? In that tale, an evil yet sickeningly sweet enchantment had befallen a prince and princess, blinding them to a very real danger. I felt that somehow we ourselves had been bewitched.

The next morning, Frances and I met in our little office cubbyhole. She looked aghast when I told her Kathy had gone to visit Bob, even though we were supposed to pick her up the next day.

Newman had found out some disquieting things, she explained, although nothing concrete. He had also given her the phone number of a Christian woman in Brenham who might know something about them; and Frances suggested I give the woman a call before making the trip.

I decided on the spot to go immediately to Brenham, and first placed the call to Newman's friend.

A pleasant voice answered the phone. She explained that she had not had an opportunity herself to visit the colony. She also said that the group seemed rather mysterious to the townspeople, but had caused no trouble, and were quiet enough.

"Zion," according to her, was located on the outskirts of town, a rundown estate belonging to an eccentric but harmless old woman. Ostensibly this woman had joined the group and was allowing them to use her property.

Newman's friend said she couldn't accompany me to the commune that particular morning, but suggested I stop by her home beforehand for prayer. I saw no point in that kind of delay and politely declined.

But when she asked if she could pray with me over the phone, I suddenly welcomed the offer. I loved the familiar prayers in *The Book of Common Prayer*, which in my life were nearly always reserved for use during church. Only on rare and desperate occasions had I dusted it off at home to seek private aid from the Almighty.

Now I listened as this quiet Southern voice began to talk with directness and confidence to a Friend she obviously knew well. Though I can no longer remember her words, I still recall the amazement that crept over me as I realized that someone—a stranger—really cared. I wasn't ready to admit it, but I was experiencing a touch of the power of prayer.

I set off almost merrily for Brenham, some 60 miles distant. On the edge of the little town, in sight of the highway, I spotted the old derelict mansion. A handpainted sign displayed the word *Zion* for all to see. I followed the arrow up a steep hill and parked in front of the building. Other buildings sprawled around the grounds.

It was a balmy spring day and I could hear cows mooing in a nearby field. Flowers were sprinkled around the landscape and the air smelled fresh and new. In this setting, the house had an air of incongruity about it. It looked out-of-place, like a Skid Row bum wandering into a ladies' tea party. Its paint was peeling and shutters were hanging askew.

I was ushered inside by a stiffly smiling young man. Huge sheets of paint hung from the ceiling of the entrance hall. A massive chandelier with one light bulb caught my eye. In one room I could see threadbare carpets, while the floor in another room was bare wood with no hint of former polish. I could see some dilapidated sofas and settees in what appeared to be the former living room, lining the walls as they do in a doctor's waiting room, except the stuffing of these was coming out. Other than that, there was no furniture. There was an odor throughout of mold and decay.

I was kept standing in the hall while a whispered conference took place somewhere out of sight. An old woman with gray hair falling to her shoulders shuffled by in bedroom slippers and a bathrobe. As she flashed me a toothless grin, a couple of young people appeared and whisked her away before I could speak to her. I heard her grumbling as she disappeared from my view.

Who on earth could she be? I wondered. Someone's grandmother? An escapee from the local nursing home? Surely not the owner of Zion!

Yet I sensed that the latter was probably who she was. A feeling of deep sorrow began to invade me, which was not eased by the sound of singing and laughter filtering down from somewhere above.

Two young men murmuring their biblical names led me up a flight of stairs, warning me to watch for the decayed places.

"We've just been here a short while," one of them explained, "and haven't had time to fix it up yet."

The growing lump in my throat prevented any reply.

A joyful band of young people was gathered in what must have been a ballroom in days of former glory. I saw Kathy sitting in a circle with some girls, clapping her hands in time to music. She acknowledged my presence with a wink and looked serenely happy.

I felt better immediately. At least she looked healthy and normal. I don't know what I expected, but I was relieved.

Bob was singing happily with a group of the men. There were two or three guitarists, but Bob was not playing his instrument. Perhaps he no longer had one of his own. He, too, looked happy, and gave me a half-wave and grin. I sat down in a chair offered me and observed the group.

There were between 50 and 60 present. The music was peppy and contagious. I almost felt like joining the singing. I could see the love of the brotherhood one for another. It was visible and genuine. Some of the enchantment from the night before took hold. Yet I felt a need to resist the seemingly irresistible.

"This is fellowship time before we eat lunch," whispered one of my guides during a break.

"Are all these young people from Houston?" I asked.

He looked startled.

"Oh, no, they're from all over," he said, and then moved away as if he had said too much.

The next song involved some dancing and hand-clapping. It, too, was infectious, and the room fairly bounced with good will. Bob's joyful countenance held my eye. I watched him as he sang and danced with his newfound friends.

Maybe this thing is truly God's purpose for him after all, murmured my wandering thoughts soothingly. *I need to accept that and stop fighting Him.*

Immediately I relaxed and began to enjoy the day. While the "Children" were eating lunch picnic-style on the floor of the ballroom, I saw for the first time the group that I decided must be the leaders. They were in an alcove off the big room, seated at a table—a sober, no-nonsense bunch.

From where I was seated, it appeared that they had a better menu, were slightly older—probably in their late twenties and early thirties—and were bent on studiously ignoring me. Their eyes would not meet mine.

Bob came over with some others and introduced me, using all biblical names.

"My name is Ahaz," he said, almost shyly.

"Ahaz? I don't know about him," I said. I had expected some name like David or Joshua—someone of some importance, anyway.

"He's a king in the Old Testament," he explained. "You can read about him in Isaiah and other places."

A bad king, I found out later.

Kathy flitted by and informed me that she wanted to stay at least until tomorrow, as originally planned. She said she loved it up here. I delayed giving her an answer.

Meanwhile, it was announced that the "babes" class would meet in the boys' dorm at 1 p.m. And after some consultation, it was decided that I would be permitted to attend. Bob and Kathy were both part of the "babes" class. I recognized another girl, Linda, but had no chance to talk to her.

The "dorm" was low-ceilinged—probably a former chicken house—and we soon moved outside, to my relief, and sat in a semicircle on the ground in front of the teacher.

He was in his late twenties, nice-looking, very articulate and extremely authoritative. He told me later that he had taken a master's degree from the University of California at Berkeley.

I had never heard anything like his message. He spoke from a literalist/fundamentalist point of view on the subject of "The Time of the End." My own sketchy Bible background found me grossly unprepared. I knew little of the "end times" and cared even less.

With the ease of a polished magician, he selected passages out of both Old and New Testaments to back up each of his extreme statements. According to him, Scripture predicts the future with one hundred percent accuracy; and though there have been many warnings in past centuries that the end was near, none of them could be proven by Scripture. Now, however, the falling away predicted by Paul in Thessalonians was proven to be *this* generation.

His voice of doom ground on and on, and I looked around at the circle of vulnerable, believing young faces drinking it all in, taking notes, nodding their heads and murmuring in agreement. He described dramatically and effectively the ills of modern society, but called America the sole culprit.

Kathy, thankfully, was nodding sleepily. I could see she was bored stiff. Bob, on the other hand, looked absorbed. It didn't seem possible to me that this could be attracting him. And the light, fresh air now felt heavy and choking. I wanted to go home.

After an interminably long talk, the meeting dispersed. Most of the "babes" hurried off to take care of various chores. So I had a chance to ask the leader a question.

"I noticed that in describing the many things wrong in the world today," I said, "you laid the blame on America for—"

"Yes," he broke in. And then he almost chanted, "America, America is at fault, America is due to die. Her materialism, education and emphasis on science is all wrong. America is what is wrong."

Bob heard this, but I could see that whether or not he agreed, he was more concerned with the fact that I had dared to question. Wanting to keep communication lines open with my son, I dropped the subject.

"Bob, I'd like to talk to you alone," I said reasonably.

He looked embarrassed, but spoke firmly. I could tell it had been rehearsed.

"Mother, I'm part of this brotherhood now. Whatever you have to say to me can be said in front of them, too."

There were four or five still standing around, who smiled at me lovingly. I felt an outsider, outnumbered.

"Well, what are your plans?" I ventured lamely.

"To stay here," he said.

And there seemed nothing more to say.

"I'm taking Kathy back today," I said. He didn't argue, nor did she when she heard the news. Suddenly she seemed ready to go.

A number of them followed us to the car after Kathy got her things. A few more gathered, singing and dancing and praying. The scene began to resemble some kind of mysterious medieval rite, lovely and gentle—the girls in full-length dresses, their hair floating in the breeze, chanting sad songs. The young men looked like gallant, tender knights, some of them kneeling, others standing with arms touching each other's shoulders, swaying slightly to the music.

At one point I saw Kathy on her knees and several laying their hands on her head. She seemed to be pleading with them or someone for something outside of her reach. I was getting a strong inclination to break it up when she disengaged herself from the group and stumbled over to me, tears streaming down her face.

"Oh, Mom, don't make me go back to the pit. Please, please—I don't want to go back to the pit."

"The pit?" I repeated, unable to grasp what she was saying. "What on earth is the pit?"

"The world, Mom, the world," she cried, with real agony on her face.

"Get into the car this instant," I hissed in a voice only she could hear. My hand tightened on her arm, and I propelled her into the car with as much force as I could muster without alarming the still-chanting "Children."

Bob moved toward us in slow motion, still singing. By the time he got there, I had the motor going, managed a brave goodbye smile, and took off down the hill, gathering speed. I couldn't get out of there fast enough.

Kathy cried almost all the way home.

"The world is the pit, Mom, and I'm not safe in it. The devil is trying to get me. I wanted to receive the baptism of the Holy Spirit to protect me. But I couldn't—I couldn't. Please take me back, please, please."

She fell asleep exhausted as we hit the outskirts of Houston.

Good God, I thought. *Is this really happening?* I was drained, depleted and completely bewildered.

7

When the Whole House Shook

The telephone was ringing as I walked into the house. Its sound seemed to meld into Kathy's words that were still ringing in my head—*I wanted to receive the baptism in the Holy Spirit . . . but I couldn't, I couldn't.*

I lifted the receiver and heard Frances Ryan's calm voice ask me what had happened that day. Like an instant replay, I found myself recalling an earlier conversation with Frances and its subsequent effect on Bob.

When Frances had shared her story with me some time before, she had described receiving something called the baptism in the Holy Spirit. As she had outlined it in a most natural and beautiful way, I had accepted it without any real question.

Then there had been those stories in the newspaper about the "Jesus people," mostly the young, who had found a joyous ecstasy in the Spirit.

Today, more than ten years later, Christian bookstores are flooded with Pentecostal and charismatic experiences based on the baptism in the Holy Spirit (which happened first to the disciples in the second chapter of Acts); but in 1971 it was new to average churchgoers like Tom and me. I took it all in like a child hearing a fascinating bedtime story.

The new inner light and peace and love shining from Frances touched me and others in our office. Yet I had no desire personally for any such experience, nor even to delve into it more fully—which was odd, considering my normally insatiable curiosity about the unknown and mysterious.

Frances, to her credit, had never tried to indoctrinate me with her beliefs. She simply told me about her own new life and let it go at that. I could see the results with my own eyes; they were impressive. She did not treat this new Way as mysterious or strange. She saw it as natural and right. I saw the outflow of God's love in her just splashing over onto those put in her path, which helped me to accept it all with ease.

Though she had had no prior knowledge of the Scriptures, Frances was now absorbed in Bible study any spare moment she had. Daily she amazed me with the practical application of Bible verses that seemed to come to her mind at a moment's notice. Far from being pious or overbearing with the way she expressed these insights, she was totally believable. Her bright, quick mind was being sharpened before my eyes, and I found myself wanting to learn more.

One time Frances had planned to take a trip, but overslept when her alarm failed to go off. Instead of the normal disappointment one would expect at such a sudden change in plans, she awakened with the strong impression that there was something more important to do. She felt she was to take a certain book to Bob to help him in his faith walk.

She tried to shrug it off, but the thought kept returning. Finally, as an act of obedience, she did bring the book to Bob late that same morning—it was *Face Up with a Miracle*, by Don Basham—with instructions for him to read a certain chapter.

That evening, dozing in front of the TV, I was awakened by a gentle hand on my shoulder, and the glowing face of my son a few inches from my face.

"Mother, the most marvelous thing," he whispered. "Jesus has baptized me in the Holy Spirit. Alone, in my own room."

His eyes glistened and his voice was tremulous, yet I saw a peace and confidence in him that spoke of a deep inner serenity.

"It's true, Mom," he went on, when I didn't answer right away. "It's real. Right now in this century, just like at Pentecost."

His joy was fresh, contagious, and I found something in my spirit responding to him. Again, as with Frances' spiritual experience, I didn't question anything; I just accepted it. How strange for me to react that way!

"Mother, you can receive this right now," said Bob tenderly, lovingly. "Let me pray with you."

But I shrank back, turning him down as politely as I knew how. It was fine for him and Frances. They seemed so happy about it. But I wanted no part of it.

I have never kept a diary, but Tom has kept a business diary for years. He uses it mostly to record business activities, but occasionally he includes notations of important family happenings. It has helped me immeasurably in keeping the sequence of events straight while compiling this book. I only wish his words reflected more of what goes on inside him.

His diary for that day, February 20, 1971, noted simply this:

Bob experiencing Pentecostal manifestation.

"Frankie," said Frances solemnly the next day, "I have never failed to pull out that alarm clock pin far enough. I don't pretend to understand it, but I believe my hand was stayed. For some reason, this must have been God's perfect timing for

Bob to read that chapter. My small part was to bring the book over when God wanted me to do it. Bob's heart must have been uniquely prepared to receive what is available for every believer."

"For *everyone*, Frances?"

"For every believer," she repeated emphatically.

But if the baptism in the Holy Spirit was available for every believer, as Frances had claimed, I wondered now what was blocking Kathy. And why was there so much fear and desperation in her?

And if it was so right, how did Bob happen to be up there in that strange place? And why was he sitting there placidly, apparently approving the kind of talk against his country that smacked to me of Communist propaganda? If that experience tended to make one weird, who needed it? I had the uneasy feeling that an unholy spirit had invaded our lives, instead of a holy one.

Remembering the excesses of some "holy rollers" I had seen as a child in east Tennessee, a sliver of fear shot through me. What had we gotten into?

All of these thoughts were churning around in my head as I picked up the phone after my trip to Zion. Settling down, I briefed Frances quickly on the day's adventure.

Kathy came into the room still crying after her sleep, and Frances asked to speak with her. They talked awhile, and Kathy began to calm down. Then Frances invited us over to her house for the evening.

Frances' home is like a haven. It is a small house, but neat and comfortable—a place where you can walk in and feel immediately at home.

When we got there after supper, her children were in bed. There were candles and soft lamplight. The night seemed to be enveloped in warmth and quietness. Kathy sank down on the living room carpet and beamed a blissful grin. She was apparently peaceful again.

Newman arrived soon after. Ever since I had met him, I had thought of Newman as a biblical character with only one name, New-man—so appropriate. He was comfortable to be with. In fact, neither he nor Frances seemed to be in a hurry about anything. I felt myself relaxing gratefully. I hadn't realized how wound up I was.

Newman prayed in a pleasant, thoughtful voice, and I sensed peace, a Presence, and the knowledge of Love around us and in us. He also prayed for God's guidance for Bob.

Newman's trust in the faithfulness of the One he spoke to touched me and rebuilt some of my own dwindling faith. The belligerence in me seemed to dissipate.

I don't remember that we discussed the Children of God situation much that evening. I guess I wanted to put it out of my mind for the moment, and Frances and Newman were given the wisdom to know and respect that.

And Kathy seemed perfectly at ease with Newman. He asked her gently about her relationship with Jesus Christ. She told him about how she had accepted Jesus as her Savior that week on the sidewalk in front of our house.

As they talked, I kept remembering her as a baby—the healing service in the Episcopal church on Long Island, and her recovery from the congenital hip dislocation. I also recalled how she used to carry a little box around with her when she was about four—her "friendship box," containing little trinkets precious to her. She wanted it with her always, she said, so she could be ready to share the contents with someone who was lonely or in need.

Another time, around age five, she announced out of the

blue that she could see God. My startled expression brought forth this explanation—that when love passed between two people, she could "see" Him.

Oh, my darling, I remember thinking, *you've known Him a long time. If this is your first mature commitment to Him, so be it, but you've known Him before.*

Now I heard her telling Newman quietly that she, too, wanted to receive the baptism in the Holy Spirit.

Newman opened his Bible and began to show her the scriptural basis for this event. He began in the Old Testament, explaining that God had often communicated to Israel through some anointed leader like Moses or David who spoke His word to the people. But then in Joel 2, God promised that His Spirit would be poured out on *all* flesh. Later, John the Baptist pointed to Jesus as the One who would baptize with the Holy Spirit.

I knew I had heard that before, but then Newman read John's words: "I baptize you with water for repentance, but he who is coming after me is mightier than I, whose sandals I am not worthy to carry; he will baptize you with the Holy Spirit and with fire" (Matthew 3:11, RSV).

It seemed I was hearing it for the first time.

Then he pointed out several verses in which Jesus told the disciples to wait in Jerusalem for power from on high—the Comforter, the Counselor, the Holy Spirit (all one and the same Person, of course).

I was struck by the fact that after Jesus' resurrection, He breathed on them and said, "Receive the Holy Spirit" (John 20:22). And yet just before He ascended, He told them to wait in Jerusalem until He sent "the promise of His Father" upon them and they were clothed with power from on high (Luke 24:49).

He had already breathed the Holy Spirit into them, and yet they were to wait to receive even more of Him? I tried to put all this into my own frame of reference.

Then, as if reading my mind, Newman spoke to this very point.

"Every born-again Christian," he said, "has the Holy Spirit with him. Yet Jesus commanded His disciples, who had already received the Holy Spirit, to wait to receive the indwelling of the power from on high in order to go forth as witnesses. I think we can look on this as an entering of the Spirit already with us, an *empowering for service* and for living the Word of God."

On he went, reading the familiar verses of Acts 2 in which the first Christian Pentecost is described. Referring to the prophecy from Joel, in which God promises that His Spirit will be poured out on all flesh, Newman continued:

"The beginning of the fulfillment of that prophecy began on the Day of Pentecost, and continues to this very day. Peter, under the power of the Holy Spirit, spoke these words to the thousands there right after he and the others received the baptism in the Holy Spirit: 'Repent, and be baptized . . . and you shall receive the gift of the Holy Spirit. For the promise is to you and to your children and to all that are far off, every one whom the Lord our God calls to him.' That means it's also for us today! We, His people, can receive right now."

Newman continued speaking quietly and with conviction.

"Actually, this power is lacking and needed in the Church today. And all the gifts of the Spirit are given, not just for individuals, but to build up the Body of Christ, the Church."

He must have seen an unspoken question in my eyes, since he addressed me for the first time.

"Frankie, would you read Luke 11:9-13 out loud?"

It was about asking and receiving. And as Newman went on

telling Kathy briefly about the gifts of the Spirit, the last verse of the passage reverberated in some chamber of my mind:

"If you then, who are evil, know how to give good gifts to your children, how much more will the heavenly Father give the Holy Spirit to those who ask Him?"

Had I been unconsciously blaming this experience of the baptism in the Holy Spirit for Bob's present predicament? The words of that last verse flowed over an inner wound and caressed it.

Kathy was kneeling in front of Newman. Frances moved over, and they both put their hands on her head and prayed for her to receive what she was asking for. Softly these "elders" began speaking lovely melodious words that rose and fell in tones of great beauty. Their hands rose slowly in praise. Through a blur of tears I saw my daughter raise her hands, and heard her sweet voice join them in praising God in a way new to her.

Newman beckoned to me.

"You can receive, too," he said gently.

I shook my head. I couldn't speak. Perhaps it was right for Kathy. But I still had some sorting out to do.

On the way home, we were hushed. Kathy broke the silence, wonder and awe in her voice.

"Mother, did you feel the whole house shake?"

I didn't answer, although she didn't notice. It had not shaken for me. Yet I knew something important had happened—for me as well as for her. The world I had always known seemed to be developing another dimension—a reality that was new and yet strangely familiar. Was I glimpsing some "other world"?

In the deep inner recesses of myself I could detect a faint stirring.

8

Bewilderment Time

Tom was waiting up for us and listened patiently as Kathy whizzed through a brief description of the past two days. She was eager for bed. After she retired, I gave him a quick resumé of my own day, wanting to go into more detail, but feeling somehow that the time wasn't right.

Tom's face was unreadable. Sometimes I caught a faintly quizzical look tinged with wonder as Kathy and I related our stories. I was grateful for his stability and calmness, although a bit frustrated by his lack of reaction.

"I think we need to sleep on all this," he said at last, with a slight grin and yawn. He wanted no discussion now, I could see.

Overall I felt relieved. At least some of the burden had shifted. Overwheimed with lassitude, I was able to fall into a deep slumber almost immediately.

The next morning, Saturday, we were all at the breakfast table when the phone rang. Tom got up to answer it and soon came back looking grave.

"That was Linda," he said, "the girl you said you recognized at Brenham. She says she's escaped. Sounds rather distraught.

She's at her parents' now and can't come over today, but she wants to talk to us as soon as possible. She's planning on going to the F.B.I. It all sounds strange and extreme."

Tom stood there in deep thought. "Frankie, I'm going to see Bob right now. Alone. I need to find out for myself what this is all about."

I was delighted. Maybe, just maybe, Bob might come back with his father.

The day passed slowly, until at last Tom reappeared, alone. He looked as bewildered as I'd ever seen him.

"I don't know what to make of it," he said wearily. "Bob looks fine. He's in good spirits. But he's adamant about staying there."

When Tom had arrived at Zion, he told me, he'd been admitted into the mansion and told that the elders were in a meeting and unavailable, but that he could talk to his son. He waited for Bob in the living room on one of the couches with its stuffing oozing out. Lots of kids were coming in and out of the room. Some found old chairs or sat on the floor, studying. All had little books tied around their necks on leather thongs, the object of their study.

When Bob appeared, he and Tom went outside together and leaned on a rail fence as they talked. The country air was fresh and clean. There were groups of kids nearby, but not close enough to overhear their conversation. Bob seemed at ease, not at all defensive: a peaceful pastoral scene.

Tom asked Bob about something Linda had mentioned over the phone—having to sign a paper agreeing to mail censorship. Bob readily admitted this was so, but explained it away by saying that so many of the "babes" had been on drugs that the elders needed to watch the mail for the kids' own good, so that pushers and old contacts wouldn't be able to tempt them.

Then Bob went into a lengthy explanation of the theory of giving up, or "forsaking," all worldly possessions in order to grow closer to God, and to show the depth of one's commitment. He didn't know what became of their "things," but shrugged it off as being of no consequence to him. It was a relief, he said, not to be burdened with them.

Bob felt he had learned more of the Bible in that week than in his entire life put together. That was important to him. The little book around his neck held Scriptures for memorizing.

"I add some every day," he explained, "and remove those I've really learned. As for America, you have to admit there's plenty wrong with it."

Bob would only nod in agreement when Tom cited America's virtues, including the freedom they had just to stand there and discuss it.

Tom said to me now, "I'm sure Bob wants us to just lay off. Yet I sense there's something wrong with the whole setup. I'm just not sure what—it's elusive." Tom was tired, physically and emotionally.

"Bob's bound to get fed up with it," he added. "Maybe we ought to just lie low."

I heard the wisdom in Tom's words, but wondered if I was ready to entrust my son to anyone's care—even God's.

Tom's diary entry for that day was less cryptic than usual:

Drove to Brenham to visit Bob. He admits some of the things Linda suspected, but is so caught up in the group that he is immovable. I'm suspicious and confused. How can the Holy Spirit be there if the intent of the group is evil?

Linda is a pretty, pert girl with a lively mind. She looked solemn and grim as she sat in our living room and described how she had gotten involved with the Children of God.

"A bunch of us, including Bob, went to Milby Park for this rock concert," she began. "Then this bus called 'the Prophet Bus' pulled up, and all these kids poured out and began to rap with us. We knew Bob had had some kind of religious experience recently, so it didn't surprise us too much when he seemed really taken up with their ideas. I began to listen, too, when Bob agreed with them about how bad the 'establishment' was and how we really weren't Christians unless we were willing to get rid of all of the material things that cluttered our lives."

I knew Linda to be of an independent nature. She had gotten a job and her own apartment; but now her face revealed bewilderment as she paused for a moment.

"I really can't explain how it happened," she went on. "All of a sudden my life seemed awfully dull. I didn't like my job. The apartment manager was giving me a hassle all the time. So when Bob said he was going with the Children of God, I just decided to go, too. Just like that.

"And at first it was great. I love to sing, and there was lots of that. But the food was awful. And they had so many moronic rules."

With that she launched into a list of grievances about the study required, the strict discipline, and how the "elders" got all the good stuff that was forsaken and the "babes" were left with the dregs.

We could see why it would be irritating to her, but none of it sounded too serious to us. I found myself wishing wistfully that Bob was having her "normal" reaction to everything. Yet I knew he was earnest about his commitment to the Lord, and guessed from what Linda said that she was not. That undoubtedly had some bearing on their differing attitudes.

Not only was there mail censorship, but phone calls were censored, too. Linda described how they had to do everything by twos, like the disciples in the Bible. It was obvious to us that the COG leadership had hit upon this method as a way to keep an eye on their "babes" and to keep their new converts in line.

She told us how she had pretended to get everything she could out of her parents over the phone, as her "guard" stood by prompting her. Then, after giving directions about where to bring her stuff, she yelled before her parents could hang up, "Help! Come and get me! I want out of here and they won't let me go."

The leaders, she said, were furious, but decided she was expendable, having been there only a week, and having the "wrong" attitude. So instead of shipping her to a colony in another location, they decided to let her go.

Linda had tried to talk Bob into leaving with her, she added, but he wouldn't listen at all.

She told us that the "lesson" I had sat in on while visiting the colony in Brenham was a toned-down version of their usual teaching. Her voice tightened in anger.

"The leaders sound like a bunch of Commies. They hate America. They teach every day that we should hate our country and our parents, and that our parents have betrayed us by giving us godless schools, Christless churches, and teaching us to worship a heartless mammon."

"Does Bob believe that?" I wondered out loud.

"I don't know. He hears what he wants to, I guess. He spends most of his time memorizing Scriptures. I can't understand him anymore."

We learned other disturbing things from Linda. The old woman I had seen was, in fact, the owner of the house. She had supposedly had a vision telling her to give her estate to the Children of God after she saw them on a TV show. Linda said they called her "Mother Zion," took good care of her, but would not allow the "babes" to talk to her. Linda felt that the old woman, like the recruits, was a sort of prisoner in her own home.

Besides this local group, we learned there were national colonies from California to New York, and all were growing fast. The leader was a man named David Berg, who called himself Moses David. The only things the Children were allowed to read were the King James Version of the Bible and the letters of Moses David, called "Mo" letters. She characterized these as strange—messages of hate and bitterness, with occasional dirty words.

"I did go to the F.B.I. yesterday," she went on, "and they were interested. They asked me questions for a couple of hours. They're particularly curious about where the money comes from, but I had no idea. Will you go to the F.B.I., too? Since you've been out at Brenham, it would give credence to my story."

After Linda left, my heart spiraled downward. I found myself reaching for a cigarette, a habit I had tried unsuccessfully for years to break. Tom and I discussed it and decided not to go to the F.B.I. We didn't have anything of consequence to report, we reasoned. Besides, we wanted to keep all avenues to Bob open. If he heard we had "betrayed" him and revealed our lack of trust in his judgment, we knew we would have cut off any hope of future communication.

Coming up several weeks later was a most special family event: the marriage of our second daughter, Susan, to her beloved Andy.

By this time Bob had been moved to another Children of God colony—a ranch near Mingus, Texas, which we later learned was owned by an admirer of David Berg. So we phoned there to arrange for him to come home for his sister's wedding.

But a strange-sounding Bob talked to us, subdued and evasive. He did not think he could come. Then we heard a whispered consultation before Bob returned to the phone.

"I cannot come," he announced, his voice now strong, "because I am about my Father's business."

And the phone went dead.

Tom and I were deeply concerned. What could we do to bring him home?

Bob wrote us a few times from Mingus, but his letters exasperated me, since they were mostly Bible quotations and cryptic religious remarks. In one there was a long rambling dissertation about nets—how he had been trapped all his life in smelly, life-suffocating nets (the world's trappings), but now he was free. Much more followed, written in vivid picture language about the world's enslavement to the wrong things.

"Life here at the ranch is Jesus Christ," he stated in one letter.

Life for Frances was Jesus Christ, too, but she had been freed from her old life in a beautiful way. Why did these same words from Bob sound so oppressive?

Later he wrote: "And, of course, the Lord is Life, everlasting and incomprehensible to the human mind. You can't understand God! You just have to trust in Him (Proverbs 3:5)."

This Scripture reference sent me searching for my old King James Bible. It was the one thing in his letter that touched a sympathetic chord, and seemed to parallel what I, too, had been learning.

"Trust in the Lord with all thine heart," I read, "and lean not unto thine own understanding." My eyes went on to verse 6:

"In all thy ways acknowledge him, and he shall direct thy paths."

Suddenly I felt furious and didn't even know why. At least, I couldn't articulate why.

On another occasion, when I was trying to think of a way to get Bob home for Susan's wedding, Newman's face kept appearing.

"Lord," I prayed, "are You turning my thoughts to Newman for a reason?"

I felt a rising excitement. Maybe it was a sign from God that Newman was the one who should talk to Bob, even get him out of the group altogether. If so, my part was simply to tell him he was the one to do it.

So I called him up. Newman listened patiently as I explained my theory to him over the phone. "Frankie, I've been praying for Bob ever since he joined that group. I'll pray about your particular request. But I need to tell you that at this point I do not hear the Lord telling me to go up there. It has been my experience that when the Lord sends a message to me through someone else, it is always a confirmation of something He is already saying to me. And I feel a 'rightness' about it. So far that is not happening in this case. Of course, He could confirm it later today or tomorrow. I know He is a God of infinite variety, and I am open to the fact that He could show me in a different way this time. But I cannot go without clear direction from Him."

I felt frustrated. I was convinced that I had been led to Newman for help, and now he could not or would not receive the message. Then I relaxed a bit, clinging to the hope that God would make it clear somehow to Newman . . . and quickly.

Before hanging up, Newman gave me some Bible verses

that bewildered me. They had to do with praising God in all situations, rejoicing in trials and tribulations. But my heavy heart had no room for praise and rejoicing. Newman must have made a mistake.

I could feel my anger rising.

My fury seemed akin to the ire I had experienced when I had looked up the Scripture given in Bob's letter, Proverbs 3:5, about trusting the Lord and not my own understanding. I was furious with Newman . . . and with Bob . . . and with the Children of God.

Or could it be that my anger was really directed against God?

When Newman called the week of Susan's wedding to say he would not be going to Mingus, I felt abandoned, and the temperature of my hot anger slipped down the scale into icy coldness.

I'll show them all that I can handle it, I thought. *And I won't include praising God in the process!*

I could almost hear myself adding, "So there!", like a little girl having a tantrum.

And so Susan's wedding bobs to the surface of my memory like a delicate, iridescent bubble, floating serenely on top of a murky pool of dark and hidden pain.

Willowy and fragile, she made a lovely bride. At the reception Tom and I waltzed to our song, "Love Makes the World Go 'Round," trying to banish from our minds the fact that an important member of the wedding party was missing. Tom's entry in his diary that night concluded, "Fine, exciting evening."

Having thus had success with keeping the pain at bay, I made a mental note to continue the practice. I would not allow myself to think about Bob—or God.

And Tom seemed to have decided the same thing, at least about Bob. We never mentioned him. It was though he had died.

9

Now, Out at the Ranch . . .

A month elapsed. Tom and I kept busy with our jobs. But when the wedding pictures arrived, distinctive and lovely, I was suddenly overwhelmed with the absence of Bob's face in them. Simultaneously, it seemed, Tom and I had the desire to go see Bob and take the pictures to show him, perhaps as an excuse for our visit.

So the following day—Sunday, July 11, 1971—we packed a picnic and set off for Mingus early in the morning. We also brought along Cozy, our poodle. Bob adored her, and we looked on her as a possible *pièce de résistance*.

It was a relief to speak about our son again. Our spirits lifted and we felt festive as we drove through the Texas countryside. We were enchanted with the name of one little town we passed through—Rosebud—and it became a kind of landmark. A petal-strewn path, we laughed.

A gas station in Mingus gave us directions to the ranch. The setting was peaceful—rolling land with graceful trees and an occasional glint of pond water through them. Then we spotted a big mailbox with the following lettering printed on it:

TEXAS SOUL CLINIC
BIBLE SCHOOL
Home of the Children of God

A formidably high barbed-wire fence surrounded the property. The four or five Children at the sturdy entrance gate reminded me of the cast from a Hollywood set for a Western movie about pioneer days.

The girls wore long calico dresses. One even wore a sunbonnet. The boys in jeans and boots looked prepared for anything, including an Indian attack. One of them held a shotgun.

Their attitude toward us was suspicious and hostile. When Tom explained that we wanted to visit with Ahaz, our son, they went into a huddle. Then one separated from the group, hopped onto a motorcycle and drove off into the ranch. We were told coldly to park our car a short distance away and to wait. Since their attitude inhibited any conversation, we did as we were told.

I was bothered by the gun. It was totally unexpected, although I suppose I shouldn't have been surprised. But I was, and Tom was, too. Though it had not been pointed at us, we had the distinct impression it was being used for one purpose: to protect the Children of God. We both sensed there was a difference in the attitude of the Children here and those who had greeted us in Brenham. The gun was an ominous symbol, and my heart was sinking once more.

The motorcycle reappeared on the horizon and bounced back to the gate in a whirl of dust. Another whispered conference. Then the young man with the grimmest face and darkest clothes ambled over to our car. Pointing to the boy on the motorcycle, he told us curtly, "Follow him."

My relief was tremendous! I had been braced for a cold refusal. Tom drove the car slowly through the gate, following our guide down a bumpy country lane into the ranch grounds. He led us up a hill to a small building with a fence around it.

"This is the guest house," he said. "Wait in there." And he drove off, once again becoming a large sound enveloped in a cloud of dust moving swiftly out of sight.

Tom and I gathered the wedding album, picnic basket and Cozy, and proceeded into the house. We were greeted by a sweet-faced young woman in a simple country frock that fell to her ankles. A silent, somber young man sat in a chair nearby. They were pleasant, but there was a hush about them that blocked conversation.

I made one attempt, asking if they knew Ahaz. She shook her head.

"Only slightly," she replied softly. "There are several hundred here. Just be seated, and he'll be along soon."

Another question was beginning to form on my lips when they glanced at each other and, as if on signal, reached for Bibles and became absorbed in study.

I began to take in our surroundings. The little house had one room with a porch, reminding me of the mountaineer cabins in the Smokies. It was clean and neat, furnished sparsely with a couch, a few chairs, and a small table or two. Although it was a warm day, in the house it was cool and pleasant.

Then the door opened and our son stepped in, accompanied by a silent young man. I was shocked by Bob's appearance.

It had been hard for us, years before, to accept the era of long hair. Because of Bob's combo, he had been among the first of his peers to embrace the Beatle look. But over the years he had modified it to the point that, though his hair was still longer than we preferred, it no longer touched his collar and was shaped becomingly. Now I realized how much I had to come to accept that look, as he walked through the door a stranger.

His very short haircut made him look severe. He was thinner than I'd ever seen him, and his face was gaunt and pale. There was a cool remoteness in his eyes and no welcome in them at all. Bob had the ascetic look of a monk or hermit, and such an air of fragility that I was almost afraid to touch him.

He did not want us to hug him—that was clear. So we didn't.

It seemed to me that his mask slipped a little when a yipping, joyful Cozy tried to leap into his arms. But it was only a momentary lapse on his part. He recovered his apparently rigid control as he patted her almost offhandedly.

I had the feeling he had shrunk. About 5'10" in height, he had always had a sturdy, solid look. He had also been blessed with quick agility and the grace of a natural athlete. Now he appeared much smaller, and was stiff and jerky in his movements.

Besides this vast physical difference, there was a subtle change that concerned me even more. Except for those years of confusion in the past, Bob had always had an air of quiet confidence, even as a little fellow. It had propelled him into leadership roles all his life. But this young man seemed uncertain and tentative in his manner, wispily dependent somehow. His teasing sense of humor was gone completely. I missed it.

"Ahaz" introduced us to the "disciple" (or guard) who accompanied him. Then Tom brought out the wedding album and Bob sat between us as we showed him the photographs. Our conversation was stilted.

All the while Cozy lay at Bob's feet, her tail beating a slow tattoo on the wooden floor. I had secretly hoped that seeing Susan's pictures would create a longing in our son to return to his family once more. But now I realized how naive I had been to harbor such a thought.

There was actual distaste in his expression, almost a physical drawing back, as if the sight of happy people dressed in wedding clothes was painful for him, a lavish extravagance compared to his now-Spartan existence. I knew then that there was no chance he would decide to come back home with us that day.

But I do not give up easily.

We asked if we could see the ranch, and after more secret whisperings, it was decided that we could see the main buildings, at least. Bob and his companion showed us around the main hall. Then we were led into the kitchen, where Bob's chores kept him most of the time. He was part of the food preparation crew, he explained, a bit of pride creeping in.

Surprisingly, he was allowed to join us for a picnic on the grounds without the "guard." My heart began to race. Perhaps there was a chance after all.

We followed Bob to a quiet shady spot under some tall trees on the bank of a shimmering pond. Except for groups of Children scattered throughout the trees, we were quite alone.

He had picked up a guitar from somewhere, and my hopes soared as he began to play some of the COG songs for us. They were different from the folk-rock we were used to hearing him play—more martial and belligerent.

When Tom asked him to sing a song he had written at age 16—a favorite of his called "What Is Love?"—Bob declined politely, explaining that he would never again sing secular songs, only songs for the Lord. I wanted to argue that point, but thought better of it when I saw Bob begin to stiffen in resistance. He had been thawing noticeably as he sang for us, and I did not want to jeopardize that.

As he continued to play, changing to songs of fellowship and brotherhood, I saw our son as a man nearly frozen to death by a severe winter storm, who had chanced upon a warm hearth and was beginning to thaw out and come back to life. But my hopes for seeing this melting completed were dashed when a young woman interrupted, not even waiting for Bob to finish the song he was singing.

"I need the guitar now, Ahaz," she ordered rudely.

Bob slipped the guitar strap off his shoulder immediately and handed the instrument to her with a gracious smile and soft, "Of course, sister." His Children of God look returned as if a switch had been flipped.

I assumed she needed it for group practice or something. In a few moments, however, she was seated near us by the edge of the pond with a young man at her feet, rasping out in a harsh voice something that could hardly pass for music.

I hated her.

"She certainly didn't show much Christian love by doing that," I remarked, an edge to my voice.

Bob looked surprised.

"She's been with the family longer than I have, Mom," he said mildly. "And I don't own a guitar anymore, remember?"

I thought I detected some smugness in that last question.

I don't recall much more about that afternoon, except my irritation with a couple who kept walking near us quoting Scripture in singsong voices. Once Bob himself suddenly intoned in a singsong voice, "I expect to see Jesus soon. He is coming in the clouds."

All Bible-believing Christians, of course, believe in the Second Coming. Episcopalians profess it whenever we repeat the Nicene Creed. But there was something eerie about the way Bob chanted it with an Old Testament prophet look about him.

Instinctively I had realized that showing too much anxiety, or begging Bob to return, would have the opposite effect from what I wanted. So Tom and I had tried to act as natural as if we were picnicking with our son on a college campus.

But it had not worked. Now I felt drained, defeated and ready to go home.

As Tom and I compared notes on the way back, I discovered that he was not as alarmed as I was about Bob's physical appearance. He thought he seemed just a little thin and peaked. Much later he showed me this entry in his diary:

Texas Soul Clinic at Mingus to visit Bob. He seems fine. Hair cut. But out-of-touch with reality. Unreachable by reason. It's good to see him so dedicated, but sad to lose his mind and spirit to fanaticism.

We hashed it over several times in the ensuing weeks, wondering if there was some approach we could try that we hadn't thought of yet. I longed to find another parent in the same boat who had found some magical solution. But finally Tom and I lapsed into silence again about Bob. We each had an open wound that was less painful if we did not prod.

Bob's letters, meanwhile, had ceased—not a word since our visit.

One day Linda showed up with an intellectual, bearded young man who was working on his doctorate in psychology. She had told him about her Children of God experience, and now he wanted to talk with us.

Jake came by several times. We liked him, and enjoyed chatting about his wanderings and the book he hoped to write. An aberration such as the strange group our son had joined sounded to Jake like another good chapter for this book.

By now Kathy was home from school and entered into the conversation with verve. After all, she had spent a night with them, and had her own perspective.

Then Jake, Kathy and Linda cooked up a trip to Mingus, because Jake was intrigued with the Children of God phenomenon and really wanted to investigate them.

I told them, only half in jest, that the three of them could end up caught in the trap, too. At the same time, I knew Linda and Kathy had had their fill of the Children of God. And Jake, with Hebrew ancestry and an inquisitive, searching mind focused on his thesis, was in no way a candidate.

We were really grasping at straws, but after checking into their plans, Tom and I agreed to let Kathy go on the unlikely expedition. We trusted Jake—and there was always that faint hope.

They returned in the wee hours of the morning, without Bob. And the next day, after they had rested, I listened to a flabbergasted Jake. At first he was almost incoherent with amazement.

"I have to say, Mrs. Brogan," he said, looking at me steadily, "they're strange—weird, even. I've never seen anything like it. I thought you and your husband might be imagining things, that maybe you were overprotective. But I don't think so now!"

They had arrived on the premises, he explained, and were taken to the guest house, just as we had been. But they had been greeted with cordiality rather than hostility.

Linda had felt she had a special mission—to reach Bob—and Jake and Kathy let her try. Kathy had spent her time fending off the proselytizing of a circle of Children chanting Scriptures and implying that the only way to salvation was joining them.

Now Jake paced the floor thinking about it, and threw his clinical detachment out the window.

"It's like they're mesmerized," he sputtered, ruffling his

hair in exasperation. "Under a spell or obsessed or something."

Jake reminded me of an angry absentminded professor, not able to keep to one subject, jumping from one thought to the next, never quite covering anything properly. "I had thought of it almost as a lark," he mused. "But it was no lark."

Strangely, instead of sinking further, my spirits were on the rise.

Someone else sees it, too, I thought. Even though it hurt to know that Bob was involved, if it could arouse easygoing, intellectual Jake to this emotional level, it meant I was not just dreaming it all up.

Jake went on to say that soon after the dialogues had started, he felt a sense of danger for the girls. Linda was making no headway with Bob, who acted like an iceberg with nothing but coldness in his eyes or manner. Linda's frustration made her cut short the time with him.

Kathy had started out deftly handling the verbal onslaughts from her peers, but soon became worn down and weary, and retreated into silence.

Jake, for his part, had tried all the debating tricks he'd polished so well in college and grad school; but this got him nowhere. Retreat seemed the best tactic. And since he felt responsible for having brought them into the "lions' den," he decided to scurry them out while there was still a crack in the gate.

When they were safely on their way in the car, he admitted to feeling vast relief.

I could identify with everything he said. I remembered my own sensations at Zion and how I had felt as my car careened down the hill, leaving it all safely behind.

"They're programmed," Jake continued, as if he were talking to himself. "They're like robots or zombies. None of it rings true. It's unreal. I don't think it's drugs, although it could be. Or hypnotism? Strange—unbelievable—weird. Brainwashed?" He had taken to muttering again.

When Kathy came in, she didn't want to talk about it or think about it or hear about it. She had covered herself with a protective shell and simply wanted to forget it. I understood that also. I, too, had tried that route.

In the early fall we caught a notice in the paper about the closing of the Texas Soul Clinic. We had been unable to find out anything about the Children of God through the media, so it came as a shock to see the bold announcement.

Tom did some checking, and found out that the ranch in Mihgus belonged to a California minister who was the founder of the American Soul Clinic. He had allowed "Moses" David Berg, the founder of the Children of God, to use the 400-acre ranch for his followers. Then the two men had had a doctrinal disagreement, and now the leaders of the Children of God were being asked to leave. The 400 Children there could stay under new direction, but all elected to play "follow the leader." No one knew where they were going.

Fortunately Tom got Bob on the phone, who confirmed the news. They were being evicted. Then Tom took off alone for Mingus. I didn't argue to go. Just the mention of such a trip made me feel exhausted.

That evening I was watching out the window when Tom pulled into our driveway, alone. He had been to the ranch and back in one day. The sadness in Tom's eyes and a brokenness in his manner answered my questions before he said a word.

This is what he wrote in his diary:

Drove to Mingus. Spent two hours with Bob. Doesn't know where he'll be moved. Won't come home. Feels like he's really living as Jesus would want.

10

The Battle of Dallas

As time went by and we heard nothing at all from Bob, a dull, aching sadness filled me that would not go away. It became a lingering grief that clung tenaciously, no matter what diversions Tom and I tried.

The tender Presence I had felt with Frances and Newman that night, and the "other world" I had glimpsed that seemed both new and strangely familiar, now seemed remote and unreachable, like a faintly remembered dream that flickered teasingly on the edge of my consciousness.

Gradually we began to see disquieting items in the paper about the Children of God. A brother kidnaped his sister out of a colony in another state and she professed much relief to have been "rescued." Another family claimed their son was mentally incompetent and had him legally removed from a Texas colony to be examined by psychiatrists. A court case seemed likely in that situation.

There was also mention of a group who called themselves FREECOG (Free Our Children from the Children of God). But kidnaping or declaring our son mentally incompetent seemed too extreme to us. Since the FREECOG group apparently endorsed that kind of activity, we were leery of joining it. Still, I longed to have another parent with whom to compare notes.

One day I noticed a classified item on the religious page of the newspaper: "If you have a son or daughter who has joined a cult called the Children of God, and you would like to meet other parents investigating it, call Mr. Able." A phone number was listed, next to the symbol FREECOG.

That seemed better, although since it was connected with what sounded to us like a radical group, we did not call. I only cut out the notice and slipped it into my billfold, where I glanced at it from time to time, wondering why I hesitated.

At last we got a letter from Bob. He was in Dallas at the Children of God headquarters. He needed money for glasses, he wrote, since his had been broken. He had them patched up so he could use them, but it was makeshift.

How desperate he must have been to break the silence and let us know where he was! And how humiliating for him to have to ask us for cash!

As Tom and I discussed whether to send money, I wondered if he would be allowed to use it for himself. Could this even be a ruse to get some money for the colony?

How suspicious can you get? I chided myself. But that question, which had just popped into my head, ballooned into a full-blown feeling of mistrust.

Tom was about to fly to New York on business for four or five days. This fact, coupled with my suspicions, spawned another idea. As I mulled it over in my head, I felt my spirits rising. Action was what I needed.

"I'm going to Dallas while you're gone," I announced to Tom that evening, "and carry the money to Bob in person. And furthermore, I'm going to convince Bob to come out of that dumb place!"

This was more like the old me—the gal who could accomplish anything she set her mind to. I felt flushed already with the anticipation of victory.

Tom was skeptical but not resistant. "Bob will be hard to persuade," he said.

"You're going to be surprised. I know I'll succeed this time."

I felt invincible, and I laid my plans well. I would not alert Bob that I was coming: a surprise attack. I would take along every one of his favorite foods as bait: peanut butter, tunafish, fried chicken, real mayonnaise, chocolate cake. I would also carry with me the newspaper clippings of the unfavorable things being said about COG as an absolute last resort, since it could backfire. I would go slow and easy, take my time, not rush anything, gain his confidence, learn anything I could about them, watch for weaknesses.

This was my battle plan. All depended on my getting in close, surveying the lay of the land, and having the wit to take advantage of every opportunity. I felt sure I could do it. I had not felt this good since it all began.

The night before "D-Day," I spotted a good omen in the newspaper. There was an announcement that the last piece of expressway between Houston and Dallas had just been opened to the public, about a four-hour drive. The way was paved, literally!

The day dawned crisp and cool—Halloween weather. I loaded my car with all the seductive picnic goodies I had prepared, and checked my purse for the newspaper clippings, Dallas map, COG address, charge cards, and plenty of money. My suitcase was packed, too. I was prepared for a long siege, if necessary. I set off jauntily for my destination with a song in my heart and no wavering of assurance.

Quicker than I thought possible, the Dallas skyline came into view. My spirits soared as I pulled off to a gas station for directions. A few minutes later, directly in front of the COG address, I drove into the only parking space in sight.

Everything was with me. In fact, I almost felt as if Someone had arranged it all. It inspired me to thank Him and ask for His continued guidance. So I did, quickly and briefly. This was "my" operation, and somehow I felt safer when I was running the show. Still, all help was appreciated.

It was a poor part of town, near the famous Cotton Bowl Stadium. Warehouses, rundown buildings, trash on the sidewalk and tough-looking people made me realize that nothing but a football game would normally have induced me to come to this area of Dallas.

The street was quiet. The number on the building in front of me was 839½, just as on Bob's letter. A steep, narrow staircase resembling a stepladder led from the sidewalk to the second floor; and at the top I could see the familiar *Children of God* sign.

With pounding heart, I climbed the stairs to the top landing where a young man was seated, tipped back on two legs of a chair, Bible in one hand, eyes closed. I could see by his moving lips and concentration that he was probably memorizing verses.

"Praise the Lord," I said softly as I stood before him. I felt like an Indian sneaking into the enemy camp and surprising the guard asleep at his post. (An Indian who knew the password, too!)

His chair thumped down on all fours and he leaped to his feet. "Praise the Lord, sister, praise the Lord!"

Recovering his composure in the process, the COG look I'd come to recognize slid smoothly down over his face. "Could I help you, ma'am?"

"I'm looking for Ahaz," I said pleasantly. "I need to speak with him."

"I doubt it can be arranged on the spur of the moment," he said. "There are a lot of us here, and we're spread all over. Is he expecting you?"

"No, I just happened to come by. But I have plenty of time," I added firmly.

He opened the door and motioned to a young woman inside. After he explained the situation to her, she ushered me in. It was an obvious waiting room, but quite large. *The guest house routine again,* I thought. Several of the Children were sitting around talking. Others were coming and going through a number of doors leading out of the room. I could also hear the sound of machinery.

"I'll see what I can do to find him," she said doubtfully, and disappeared through one of the doors.

On a nearby bench a large bearded black man was listening intently to an emaciated young man with tears running down his face. I felt drawn to them, and wished I could hear what they were saying.

There was a steady hum of activity. No one paid any attention to me. I felt anonymous, a bit like a spy who had successfully melded into the landscape.

Then a door opened and two young men deep in conversation walked in. One of them was Bob. Our eyes met and a miracle happened: I saw unabashed joy cross his face.

"Mom!" he exclaimed in astonishment. Then, in a split second, the mask fell back into place. Even so, I was overwhelmed with gratitude.

Thank You, God, thank You, I breathed. *Only You could have pulled that off, and only You knew how much I needed it.*

Aloud I said, "Hi, darling," trying to sound cool and nonchalant. "I understand you need some new glasses."

He responded with a grin. His guard was still down to some degree.

"Mom, this is Amorite. He's our band manager. I'm part of a six-piece combo now. I'm off K.P.," he added, and truly seemed more like himself. "We really have a good group—for the Lord." That was a hasty afterthought.

"I'm so glad," I replied with genuine pleasure. I knew how much his music was part of him. It had added to my hurt to see all his creativity stifled.

"Bob, your dad is in New York for a few days, so I decided to come and see what you're up to here." I tried to sound as if it were the most natural thing in the world. "I want to find a motel room nearby. Do you know where one is? And I have the cooler filled with picnic stuff."

Dismay flashed for a moment, followed by the usual secret whispered conferences with some of the others.

"I'll wait here till you work out the details," I offered graciously, then sank down on the bench again. I could scarcely believe my good fortune. It could not have gone better!

Amorite came over to chat. I liked him. He seemed more natural than any other member I had spoken with, and less infected with COG jargon and mannerisms. He could have been one of Bob's buddies from high school or college. Yet he'd been part of COG longer than Bob, I learned. It simply hadn't appeared to "take" with him.

Bob soon returned, almost animated. He wondered if I would mind transporting some of the Children to another place. And as a bonus, Bob had been given some time to spend with me for a picnic.

Without a guard? I wondered, silently and hopefully. Aloud I expressed pleasure at being able to be of service to them. We were all smiling like old friends.

Before we left the building, Bob and Amorite took me back to a room where machines were whining and clanking. They had gotten permission somehow to show me some of their operation here, and they were obviously proud of the facilities at their disposal.

This was the place where they cranked out most of their literature. It seemed to me that they had inherited the press from some old newspaper. The thing was old and noisy, but it worked. There were stacks of tracts and cartoon-like booklets in one room and a printing press doing its thing in another. Lots of busy-looking young people were typing and sorting printing materials and operating various machines.

But when I asked for some of their literature, I found I had once again gone too far. This would require permission from higher up, I was told, since much of this printed material was internal communication for members only. In fact, my guides began to wonder if they had gone too far in allowing me into the printing area at all.

So, remembering my battle plan, I squelched my curiosity, stopped asking questions, and allowed myself to be propelled toward the exit. I would not let myself be dismayed by anything.

When we reached the waiting room once more, we were met by a number of young men waiting for us. The guard on the landing was the picture of amazement as we tromped down the stairs to my car. And I felt as smug as the new kid on the block who has unexpectedly won the local hopscotch game!

As we approached my car at the bottom of the stairs, the Children gathered about it to pray for a safe journey. One of them explained that they had just had a class about this kind of prayer. They were in full accord about its necessity and the manner in which it was to be done.

Remembering my battle plan of going easy, and gaining their confidence by listening with love and interest, I felt peaceful and right in my role as observer. As they began to pray, I bowed my head and tried to enter into the spirit of what they were doing.

It was an exercise that took a while, since they mentioned many parts of the car by name—brakes, steering wheel, spark plugs, etc. They invoked the Lord's protection and took authority over the devil and his cohorts on each and every working part they could think of. Then they prayed for protection from other drivers.

It turned out that this ritual—chanted rather than spoken—was necessary every time we got into the car to go anywhere.

I discovered that, by observing this incident (and others later) from an almost detached viewpoint, with no condemnation or criticism surfacing in my face or manner, I was becoming accepted by them. I also realized that no matter how wrong the motives of my battle plan might be—I could already see they were a bit underhanded and manipulative—I was nonetheless gaining some valuable insights in the process.

In fact, to my surprise, I realized I was seeing these Children of God through eyes of love. And love was opening up vistas! It was a totally unexpected byproduct of my "method."

To me, the "car prayer" suggested not faith, but rather a lack of it. The young people appeared to be more aware of the devil's power to inflict damage than confident in God's power to protect. It also occurred to me that if they forgot to mention a particular part of the motor, or did not chant with just the right inflection, and then if the car broke down or was involved in an accident, they would consider the fault their own.

What a burden for the poor kids! I could see that a climate of fear could be created this way.

Our first stop was a huge warehouse. As several of the "brothers" disappeared through a pair of mammoth sliding doors, someone else explained that the warehouse owner had become their benefactor. He had learned that many of the

Children had no shower facilities, so he was allowing them use of the warehouse showers on a staggered schedule. The two guys I dropped off were there to take their showers. Bob's turn came the next day.

Our next stop was a large rundown house near the warehouse. Everyone except Bob got out, since they were to have a class there. Then, just as it began to appear that I was going to have Bob to myself, a pleasant-looking young man ran out and hopped into the car—the disciple-guard once more! He was our assigned companion for the picnic.

His Bible name was Zacharias, and I began to size him up as he and Bob got down to the serious business of incantation for the car's safety. He was soft and sweet, naive and innocent, simple and childlike.

And later, as he told me more about himself, I found my initial impressions were right. He had been introduced to the Bible and Jesus by the Children of God, and brought out of the drug scene in the process. His background was one of dire poverty—such a lack of material necessities and human love that he considered the COG fellowship to be heaven on earth.

When he opened the Bible to read a story from the Old Testament, his awe of the great truths there humbled me. I could see he was overwhelmed with these new discoveries. Even the reverence with which his rough hands handled the holy Book made me duck my head to hide the quick tears. I almost fell in love with him on the spot!

It was hard for me to admit, but it seemed that some young people were being helped by COG. I thought of the tender care of the black man in the waiting room for the weeping lost soul beside him. Through Zacharias I could see that God's Word can penetrate to a person's heart no matter *who* introduces it.

I had seen God's love wooing and bringing healing even in

the midst of those I sensed were in serious error. But what would happen to these vulnerable, pliable, hurting "little ones" as they received wrong teaching? This musing brought me to a place of aching questioning, with no simple answers.

After Zack (as I came to call him from my position of love) got into the car and the three of us were alone, I suggested we locate a motel for me. Bob and Zack went into prayer immediately, as if on signal, asking for guidance.

"God will lead us there," Bob intoned with the special COG inflection.

He and Zack then took turns suggesting which way we should go at each traffic light or stopsign. I followed their directions exactly and without question.

As we wandered around in some unsavory areas, and on a strange, circuitous route for 15 minutes or so, with no sign of a motel, I longed to see one for their sakes as well as my own. Then, when we stopped for a traffic light beside a service station with a telephone booth in obvious evidence, I heard myself asking if God could possibly be telling us to make use of this modern instrument to direct us.

"I'll bet that's it," said Zack, our innocent.

Bob was silent, probably irritated. But it served as a face-saving solution to the problem.

I located a nice motel nearby through the phone book. As Bob and Zack helped me carry my things into the room, I caught them glancing in the direction of the tub.

"Help yourself to the facilities, including the shower," I offered as casually as I could. I knew Bob had valued his morning shower and shampoo as the only way to begin a day.

They stopped mid-step and stared at each other.

"We'll have to pray about it," they agreed.

I left the room to give them privacy to pray, but when I returned, they had "heard the Lord." It was not to be permitted. They should not take advantage of a luxury not available to the other brethren.

It was well after noon by now, and Bob suggested a nearby park for the picnic. We drove there in minutes. It was everything I had longed for and more. The fall day was perfect, the park isolated and quiet, with busy squirrels and songbirds our nearest companions. The hum of the city and an occasional car horn were distant and remote.

The eyes of my memory see that picnic as a haunting, dreamlike sequence with everything in slow motion—a hazy interlude, peaceful and misty. I spread the white tablecloth on the grass and, with the reverence of a priestess at the high altar, placed my offerings on the cloth.

As I did, Bob and Zack became little boys set unexpectedly free, as they tossed an abandoned ball they had found under a bush. They began running, falling, then rolling around on the ground laughing with glee. True children of God!

When I motioned them to the banquet table, they came and knelt before it, awed by the plenteous spread. As they glanced shyly at each other, I felt I could read their minds.

We did not take the shower, they agreed silently, *but we have permission for this.*

Out loud they said, "Praise God for His blessings to us."

It was a holy time, a joyous time for each of us. They ate in silence, reverently, savoring each bite. I just nibbled, too full of joy to be hungry.

My cup runneth over. Please, God, let it go on.

I was afraid to speak, to break the spell.

They fell asleep in the shade and I packed up quietly. Then I watched Bob sleep. His face was unlined and vulnerable, relaxed and childlike. I longed for him to wake up, ready to go back to Houston and resume his life there. He could bring Zack, too, I mused wistfully.

Bob woke up first, his guard down. He talked softly, not wanting to disturb his friend. He told me about his music; his joy at learning the Bible; the fellowship and the discipline. I was his confidante. My "ruse" was working—temporarily, at least. I knew not to ask my question yet. Bob seemed more like himself.

Yet I felt I was walking a tightrope: one slip, and his mask would reappear and I would topple away out of reach. My heart beat fast, but I tried to appear natural and at ease. I took this opportunity to give him the money for his glasses, secretly hoping that he would be buying them in Houston.

After Zack woke up, and the subject of marriage in the commune came up, I learned to my relief that neither Bob nor Zack was eager for this step. But what I heard about the subject appalled me.

It seemed that the boys and girls were not allowed to date or get to know each other privately in any way. When a boy decided on a girl in COG, he discussed it with the elders. The girl was then notified and could have her say. If she disagreed, they usually made her "see the light"—the wisdom of God's direction through the elders.

Occasionally the elders arranged a marriage totally. They followed the civil laws and got legal marriage licenses and blood tests. The ceremony was then performed by an elder (whose legal right to marry anyone I secretly questioned).

The offspring of these marriages, I learned, were kept in one place and cared for by those assigned to the children's ministry. This sometimes resulted in the parents' having very little to do with their children's upbringing. Also, I learned about at least one set of parents who had left their children behind when they were sent off to another commune on some special mission. No one knew how long the parents and the children might be separated.

To Bob and Zack, with their COG countenances easing back into place as they discussed "the family," these parents were noble and self-sacrificing, doing God's will.

As their voices droned on, relating the hard facts, I could tell they either agreed with these practices or did not dare to question them. Gradually I became aware that the beauty of the afternoon, which now plays back in my mind like a delicately choreographed ballet, had emerged from its gentle somnolent state into harsh reality. Their masks were back in place. They had lapsed back into their jargon and COG mentality.

We were separated once more.

How did it change so quickly? I wondered, as my hopeful spirits began to sag. *Have I missed some important cue in my battle plan? Lost an opportunity—forever?*

"What time is it?" asked Bob, sounding loud and anxious. "I have to lead Inspiration Hour tonight. We mustn't be late."

So we scurried to the car like children who have been playing hooky, hoping to get back before being found out.

"I'll try to get you into Inspiration Hour," Bob whispered conspiratorially as the motor started up.

And my spirits shot up like a skyrocket. It took so little to give me hope. I grinned to myself as we wended our way through the traffic: they had forgotten the prayer routine.

Once again there was a convenient parking spot directly in front of COG headquarters. I felt I had an secret Ally, which gave me hope and courage. I decided to act as natural as possible and go in with them, as if permission had already been granted.

I still don't know if Bob actually did ask anyone. He was so preoccupied with his responsibility for leading the music that he may have simply forgotten. At any rate, I soon found myself in a huge barn of a room crowded with well over one hundred Children of God. They were just cleaning up from their evening meal, which I learned they had eaten picnic-style on the floor. The few chairs in the room were for the elders.

I sat down on the floor near Zack, trying to look invisible. The Children were relaxed, radiating happiness. The room was charged with an air of conviviality. Again, as in Brenham, I felt its contagious attraction.

After some of their singsong prayers, Bob stepped up with his guitar to the microphone at the front of the room, and "Inspiration Hour" really began. There were two or three other musicians with him, but he was the leader, drawing worship out of the group.

O Lord, do You really want him here? I groaned inwardly, close to tears. *Can he help these kids?* Bob looked so right up there, so glad to be contributing to their life together. And he was truly making a contribution; I could see that.

After a few tender, worshipful tunes and a couple of happy fellowship songs (which everyone sang with gusto), the music changed. I didn't like the shift. The group sang of being persecuted and dying for the Lord. They sang scornfully of the world and its ways. They became an army singing battle songs.

Music is a powerful tool, son, my heart cried out to Bob silently. *It should be used carefully and wisely. Oh, can't you see the wrongness here? Your gift is being misused.*

But he could not see it, I could tell. He was sure of what he was doing.

The knowledge of my inability to reach him was more than just frustrating. It was the source of a deepening sorrow—the anguish of helplessness. It was not being able to help a loved one who desperately needs aid but does not know it.

At length, a young woman in her early 30s, obviously an elder, marched out to take over the meeting. She conveyed an officious "schoolmarm" manner that set my teeth on edge at the sight of her. Her voice, sharp and demanding, also grated on my nerves.

Her role, as she saw it, was to chasten these naughty kids about their lack of diligence in study, chores, and anything else she could think of that would put them in their place.

I was amazed at the meek, sheepish, accepting faces within my range of vision. They seemed to feel that her tongue-lashing was well-deserved. Bob's face was blocked from view, but I hoped he had just turned her off. He was good at that. Perhaps these others were doing the same, but they appeared to be humble and contrite. It occurred to me that not even first-graders would react with such head-hanging shame to this kind of tirade.

Her shrill voice snapped out a question that surprised me: "How many of you are married?"

It must also have surprised them, because there was a moment of hesitation before hands went up slowly all over the room. I glanced around, astonished at the number.

Her voice lowered accusingly. "And how many of you are sitting together as husband and wife?"

Only a handful of couples could raise their hands. They wore the smug look of teacher's pets as she beamed on them.

"Then the rest of you get together—immediately," she barked in her best top-sergeant voice.

There was an embarrassed hush, no laughing or giggling, as shamefaced couples met in little twosomes all over the room.

"Don't act like strangers. You may hold hands. The Lord wants you to show affection for each other." She spoke as if they were in kindergarten and she was helping them get acquainted.

The scene sickened me. I had the squeamish feeling you might get if your dinner party hosts had an embarrassing argument in front of you at the table. My discomfort increased as I noted the ages of the wives. Many looked young and unsure of themselves.

Then I noticed Amorite, Bob's likable band manager, who was one of those being joined by a bride. She was none other than my old nemesis of the Mingus episode—the hateful girl who had snatched Bob's guitar away that afternoon by the pond. Now she looked as disagreeable as ever.

Amorite lost his casual air of contentment and detachment as she stalked over to sit beside him. He looked trapped and miserable. I felt sorry for him and wondered how that alliance had ever come into being. I couldn't believe he had chosen her.

"Now," cooed our crosspatch leader into the mike, as if she sensed she had gone far enough with this disciplinary routine. "I have marvelous news for all of you."

She waited dramatically until every motion had ceased and every tongue was still.

"Your elders have been in deep conference for more than twelve hours with the parents of a very messed-up fourteen-year-old girl. They have been unable to curb her drug habit or bring her to the Lord."

Here she paused. Every eye was on her, and no one moved.

With deliberate, measured tones, she announced, "We have persuaded them to sign her over legally to the Children of God."

Pandemonium broke loose. The kids jumped to their feet shouting, dancing, laughing, crying. But in the split second between the end of her statement and the celebration, her eyes met mine and she realized for the first time that an interloper was present.

What she saw was the stricken face of one who has just been stabbed. I felt my very heart had been pierced.

That poor child won't even have anything to say about her marriage, my thoughts bobbed in the hubbub. *I should have joined FREECOG before. I hope I still have that phone number. Parents need to be warned.*

I never took my eyes off the leader. I could see her hard face as she went over to a group of elders and nodded toward me. I no longer cared. One of the men went over to Bob and conferred. Bob walked slowly toward me, tapping Zack on the way. I could see he was angry.

"Mom," he said softly, "they think it's best if we take you back to the motel now."

Slowly it dawned on me that he was angry with them, not me.

We drove back to the motel in silence. I wasn't sure if Bob was even aware of his anger. Emotions like that had been denied him for so long.

"Won't you come in and read the Bible some for me before you go back?" I asked, desperate but clever.

It was the magic combination. His irritation with his elders and my asking him humbly to read his beloved Book did the trick. They followed me into my room.

"Zack, I believe we should take a shower now," Bob said, not realizing his rebellion was showing. "You go first."

Dear old Zack was delighted. No "guard" instinct in him at all! He was a pussycat—or a puppy dog, all frisky, friendly joy. He disappeared into the bathroom, humming happily.

"Bob, could we please talk?" I asked when we were alone.

"Nope," he said kindly but firmly. "Not now. I'm going to read to you as you asked. I thought Zack and I would take your car back tonight. Then, tomorrow morning, I'll pick you up and let you take me to breakfast. We can talk then. I won't bring Zack. Or anyone."

My heart leaped.

He's considering coming home, I thought. *Go easy, old girl.*

Bob's eyes warned me not to push him, as he picked up his Bible and began to read. Even though he read it with all the COG inflections, it didn't bother me this time—although I have to admit I don't remember anything he read. My thoughts were dancing in anticipation of possible victory the next day.

Zack appeared all pink and shiny, his hair damp and slicked down. Then, as Bob showered, Zack read me the story of David and Goliath with real awe and wonder. His childlike wonder was totally believable.

When Bob came back into the room, he seemed subdued and thoughtful.

"I've been thinking, Mom," he said slowly. "I don't believe your car would be safe in our neighborhood all night."

"I'll risk it," I said, too quickly.

"No. You'd better drive us back—that is, if you're not afraid to drive back here alone tonight. I think that would be best. Then you can pick me up in the morning." He grinned to reassure me as he said it.

I knew something had changed. I felt I had lost ground, but knew it was unwise to press him.

"Whatever you think, Bob," I capitulated.

Back in front of COG headquarters, he and Zack lingered at the car telling me goodnight. Suddenly an old man, unsteady on his feet, moved out of the shadows and came up to us.

"Please, brother," he whined, "let me join your group. You're the only good thing around here. I want to be a Chir'n of God, too."

He was an old wino in shabby clothes, with a red nose spotlighted by the streetlight. His all-but-empty wine bottle hung in one hand. He took the last swig and set the bottle carefully, elaborately against the lamppost.

"Tha's my las' drop," he announced solemnly. "Now I'm ready to be one o' you."

Bob moved over to steady him, and put an arm around him. My son's face gentled in the soft light, with the tender concern I had seen many times through the years when he brought strays home.

"Where do you live, brother?" Bob began softly, as I sat in the car and watched him and Zack minister to the man.

Then two elders who had been hidden from view at the top of the stairs decided this had gone on long enough. They hurried down the stairs, their authoritative manner swinging like a billy stick. Before I realized what had happened, they had bid me a firm goodnight, allowing Bob and Zack to do the same. I was dismissed to drive back to the motel, and Bob and Zack were pointed up the stairs.

My last glimpse of the old man's face lingered with me as I drove back and got ready for bed. There was such a poignant mixture of puzzlement, anxiety and hope mirrored there that I ached for him.

My fitful sleep was broken by a jarring ring. It was still dark in the early fall morning. As I reached for the phone by my head, I heard Bob's voice on the other end of the line.

"Mom, I'm sorry to wake you up, but I've been up all night with the elders, and I have to go get some sleep now. Mom, I love you, and I know you mean well. But this is tearing me apart. I cannot see you today, or anymore for a while. My mind is made up. I'm called to be here, and I have to be obedient to the Lord and stay."

My mind was beginning to clear. "Are you alone, Bob? Are you saying this of your own free will?"

"Yes, I am quite alone."

I believed him.

"Then let me have my say. I think you owe me that." Tears were beginning to surface. I could no longer hold them back.

He agreed, and for the next half-hour listened patiently to a mother's anguished concern for her man-child. I used every argument I had been piling up carefully through the months, plus a few new ones I had garnered from my close observations of their colony.

I asked about the old man, and learned that the elders would not consider letting him join, since he would not "fit in." It seemed like a trump card to me, so I leaned heavily on the lack of Christian love revealed by that alone. It also allowed me to point out that they were evidently not trusting the Lord's ability to change the man.

Finally Bob was also tearful, and weary.

"Mom, I know we're not perfect. Maybe part of the reason the Lord wants me here is to help correct that. Nothing you can say is going to sway me. This is pure torture for both of us. Please let me go."

The battle was lost. I could faintly hear the bugle sounding retreat.

I told him I loved him. That we, his family, loved him. That he was welcome home anytime. He told me that he loved me—and Dad—and all of us. We said goodbye to each other. And the phone clicked into silence.

I wept until there were no tears left.

11

Waving the Lantern

After I had regained my equilibrium from the painful defeat in Dallas and mournful drive back home, I contacted FREE-COG, and Tom and I joined their ranks.

We were welcomed with open arms. Our fresh input was valuable to them. It seemed I had been allowed a closer look into the COG inner sanctum than most of the other parents. I wished now I had kept notes. As a spy, I was a flop. I had only memory and impressions to rely on.

We met other parents who lived near us whose children had been in COG eighteen months to two years. One family lived only two blocks away on the same street.

Though we had been exasperated by Bob's refusal to come to our daughter's wedding, we now learned of another family whose experience was more shocking. Their young daughter at home had died unexpectedly. Griefstricken, they called their son in COG, expecting him to come home for the funeral. "Let the dead bury the dead," was the cold reply that ended their conversation.

After our months of loneliness, we found it helped to share stories and experiences with other parents undergoing the same kind of ordeal. I suppose there was a certain element of the "misery loves company" syndrome, but the main impact FREECOG had upon us was one of relief to have hard facts at our disposal after the months of suppositions.

We learned that there were other FREECOG chapters, or similar parent alliances, in large cities all over the United States. An information exchange program between these groups was most helpful.

And our fears that FREECOG was a radical group were soon quieted. Whenever parents who believe their children are being threatened in any way gather for support, there exists the potential for a volatile, emotional situation. In this group, however, we were impressed with everyone's levelheaded, intelligent approach. Pains were taken to examine data carefully, sifting fact from rumor. Those in leadership roles took their jobs seriously.

Our chapter of more than fifty families represented a wide cross-section of society, ranging from rich to poor and from highly educated to barely educated. We were white, black and brown; Protestant, Jew and Catholic, as well as "religionless." We had one mark in common: we all had an ache inside, reflected in our eyes. Some couples sent only one member to the meetings, the other being too spent emotionally to attend.

Through the ensuing weeks, Tom and I attended FREECOG meetings together and lent our talents to help. Tom helped prepare information for newspapers and internal FREECOG communiques. I appeared on a television show, and later on a radio talk show.

Once, when asked why I was so concerned over a son who was over 21, I replied: "When you know a train is rushing full-speed toward a trestle over a chasm at night, and you know the trestle is down, you run out with a lantern to stop the train. You don't have to know who is on the train, much less how old they are."

I did not say it, but I no longer had much expectation of being able to convince Bob to leave. I had tried my best and failed. It was now the memory of the young girl legally signed over to COG by her ignorant parents that spurred me on to try to inform others of the true nature of the cult. I had to wave the lantern. That's what FREECOG was all about.

And what was this danger? We could see it through the accumulation of facts as pieced together from several sources. In all, it could only alarm us.

The founder was a man named David Berg. (He had adopted "Moses" as his biblical name in COG, but was also known as "Mo" or "Father David.") Berg had at one time been a minister of the Christian and Missionary Alliance. Somewhere along the line, a congregation for whom he had helped raise money rejected him and his doctrines. In anger he had, in his own words, "declared war on the g—d— system!"

David Berg, his wife Jane (or "Eve"), and their four married children and mates formed the nucleus of a small commune in southern California known as "Teens for Christ." Around 1969 they began to call themselves the "Children of God." Helped by J. Fred Jordon, a Los Angeles television preacher (who owned the ranch at Mingus), and further aided by an NBC television exposure, the small sect ballooned into a national phenomenon.

At the time we joined FREECOG, David Berg's whereabouts had become something of a mystery. But the colonies, which had popped up from coast to coast and even spread to Europe, were held together by a common thread—"The Moses ('Mo') Letters." These letters continued unabated, and influenced the daily affairs of the farflung colonies.

One definition of a Christian cult is a "sect that professes belief in the gospel plus something else." The Children of God's "something else" was, and still is today, the "Mo" letters. These were required study for all COG members.

Often Children of God converts could be seen on street corners handing out or selling pamphlets. These, for the most part, were the "Mo" letters intended all along for the public.

But FREECOG provided us with some copies of "Mo" letters of a different ilk. These were meant for COG eyes only. Smuggled out by escaping COG members, they had been verified as authentic by the *Seattle Post-Intelligencer* newspaper whose reporter had interviewed the three sect leaders mentioned in them, including one of Berg's own daughters.

The letters were damning evidence of techniques COG used to manipulate the so-called "System," or establishment. They were permeated with a tone of hate and conspiracy against anyone not in their inner circle, their elite group. The writing itself was punctuated with curse words and sexual innuendo, and revealed throughout a deep bitterness and hatred toward "enemies" who "Mo" thought had wronged him—the Church and America.

Tom's comments in his diary stated it this way:

Studied COG material. It's an unbelievably insidious plot. More convinced than ever we should get Bob out of there.

After reading FREECOG's information, whenever I thought of David Berg a picture flashed into my mind of the Pied Piper of Hamlin. I could see him piping his merry tune. But the same notes that lured the rats out of their hiding places to the river, where they were drowned, now beguiled the children away from home and loved ones as they followed the Piper, dancing, unaware of any danger.

I had always been bewildered by that fairy tale as a child.

The meaning had seemed unclear. Now the horror of it seemed all too real, and very clear.

There was a lovely bonus in joining FREECOG—some deep and lasting friendships. I was drawn in particular to two mothers, Rose Marie and Charlsie, who also had sons in the cult. Their sons had been involved much longer than Bob (eighteen months or so). Though not giving up the battle, these two had come to a kind of acceptance of the situation that reflected in their manner. There was an appealing peace and inner sureness about them.

Some of the other parents were so filled with anger and bitterness that their lives were becoming corroded with suppressed hate and rage. I watched Rose Marie and Charlsie minister to these hurting ones with compassion. They reached out to me, too, and I was comforted and encouraged by them.

I learned that both of them had been brought to their knees through the apparent loss of their sons, each in her own way coming into a deeper relationship with God. The light and love I had seen in them was no illusion. They were reflecting a life and strength beyond them that came, I gathered, from an empowerment by the Holy Spirit.

Though still confused by this Christian concept, I saw a wisdom and maturity in these two women that I desired for myself.

Rose Marie and Charlsie had had more firsthand contact with the cult than the rest of us had. When their sons had been drawn into COG nearly two years earlier, the parents had believed at first that the Children of God was a fine Christian group. They had befriended these young people by letting big groups of Children and elders stay at their homes before they were settled in a colony.

Soon both women, along with their husbands, began seeing things that disturbed them. There was a secretiveness about the elders that was out of character for an open Christian fellowship. They were dismayed at the way certain Children, called "procurers," were being trained to solicit funds from businessmen. The methods they used were sly, slick, and in most cases downright dishonest. Also, these parents were appalled at the anti-American propaganda.

Questioning the elders about these things led to more secrecy and cooler relationships. Eventually the situation deteriorated, until finally the Children left. In each family the son was deaf to his parents' warnings, and departed with the Children of God. Desiring to keep contact open, neither family had allowed a harsh confrontation, yet each had expressed their disapproval to both elders and sons.

Among other things, FREECOG had developed a list of practical suggestions for parents who might be in contact with their "captive" ones. One of these suggestions said: "Know your Bible. It could help counter their twisted learnings with the true meaning of Scripture."

I could see the wisdom in that, since I had been often aware of my own lack of Bible knowledge. When confronted by Bob or other Children with their interpretations that rang false to me, I had felt irritated and impatient with myself because I didn't know enough to refute them.

Thus, on my own, I began to study my long-neglected King James Bible. It became a frustrating experience. So much of what I read seemed to support what they were saying. There appeared to be a stern quality, almost a harshness, in many verses—especially concerning discipleship—that I had never detected in the New Testament.

For instance: "Think not that I am come to send peace on

earth: I came not to send peace, but a sword. For I am come to set a man at variance against his father, and the daughter against her mother, and the daughter-in-law against her mother-in-law. And a man's foes shall be they of his own household" (Matthew 10:34-36).

It seemed to me that each time I picked up my Bible, confident I would discover something helpful—some words that would confound Bob and open his eyes to the error of his ways—I would stumble instead upon one of these hard, uncompromising statements from Jesus Himself. There was no mistaking the red lettering in my Bible.

I discussed my problems with Charlsie and Rose Marie, who each offered to take me to Bible classes they knew about, but I balked. Such classes sounded too extreme. The Episcopalian side of me feared what I thought of as "fundamentalism."

One day when the three of us were talking, I sighed my relief about the apparent puritanical sexual attitudes upheld in the COG colonies, as compared to a "hippie" commune currently in the news that proudly proclaimed the shared sex life of its members.

They agreed this was true as far as the "babes" were concerned, but indicated they had reason to believe there was a double standard concerning what was expected of the Children and the leaders' sexual behavior. Other FREECOG members reported similar revelations. Nor did the COG leaders themselves deny this. They pointed to plural marriages mentioned in the Old Testament as a scriptural basis for their behavior. Still, the practice was currently confined to the leadership level, as far as FREECOG could determine.

"What's really disturbing is the realization that this is only the beginning," said Rose Marie at one point. "It's inevitable that this attitude will eventually slip down into the ranks.

When the enemy gets his evil claws into something, it's only a matter of time until what is hidden and subtle today will become open and monstrous in the future. Satan always overplays his hand."

Rose Marie's words about Satan seemed overly emotional at the time to me, but today there is ample evidence that her prophecy was on target.

In the fall of 1971, though heartsick that our son was engulfed in a way of life we knew to be destructive, we made no more overt attempts to extract him from the Children of God.

We waited. With other FREECOG parents we waved the lantern.

And we waited.

12

Crumbling Barriers

The waiting game is always very hard for me. Now it became intolerable.

Disinterested in the real estate business, which a year ago had absorbed me; unable to find answers in the Bible on my own; helped only up to a point by FREECOG; with two of my daughters married, the third away at school and Tom pressured by his work, I looked around for help.

I heard that a group of young people called the Agape Force would be ministering to adults as well as youth one evening at the Evangelistic Temple. I went, following some urge I didn't understand.

The huge auditorium was filled with a happy mixture of young and old. There was an atmosphere of suppressed excitement, joy bubbling under the surface ready to erupt. Though it was now midway through autumn, I felt as if I were breathing the light, fresh air of spring. A surprising gladness crept into my heart. I had not realized how accustomed I had become to the bleakness of my internal state.

Expectancy was born in me. Something was about to happen and I knew it.

I did not recognize a single face in the huge throng, yet I felt one with them. I believed they felt akin to me, too. Every face that caught mine was open, smiling, friendly. Though I did not want to speak to anyone, and no one intruded with words, their eyes welcomed me.

When the singing began, we were united even more. The music, powerful and moving, ministered to us all. It cleansed, soothed and stirred us. It touched and healed and molded us even more surely into one being. I never believed I could sing well, and had never cared much for music—especially church music. Yet now I found myself joining in freely and loving it.

The words of one song that night slash through my memory and stand out starkly against my shadowy recollections. Taken from Jeremiah 29:13-14, they seemed to hold a special message for me: "You shall seek Me, and you shall find Me, when you shall search for Me with all your heart. I will be found of you, I will be found of you, when you shall search for Me with all your heart."

The meaning of that last phrase in its lovely old English flowed into my heart as a genuine promise. My God was speaking to me. A key fitted neatly into a locked door somewhere deep inside. Barriers were crumbling, even as tears rolled freely down my cheeks.

The evening swept by in a happy blur of sharing, teaching, prayer, laughter, closeness. In one long moment of holy silence, together in the hush, we experienced an all-embracing Love. This was beyond emotion. It was a touching of human spirit with the divine Spirit. In one sense I felt deeply immersed in all that was going on; in another sense I was standing outside as an awed observer.

When it was all over, I slipped out of the service and hurried home. I could see myself as a small figure beckoning to God with one hand, and holding the other hand palm out in the universal gesture of *Stop! (Please help me, God . . . but don't get too close.)*

I tried to put that evening and Bob out of my mind. Yet it seemed that reminders of both kept cropping up in the most unexpected places. My inner ear kept hearing Bob's voice singing the Jeremiah song. I could almost see his face up there with the group at the Temple. He would fit right in with them, I knew. Why hadn't the Agape Force come by first instead of the Prophet Bus? It didn't seem fair.

Once I thought I heard Bob's voice singing on the car radio. I learned I was mistaken when the announcer gave the singer's name, but I bought the record anyway. When I played the record for them, Tom and Kathy were likewise fooled by Paul Stookey (of the folk group Peter, Paul and Mary) singing "The Wedding Song."

Kathy listened to it several times, thoughtfully. Then she said, "Mom, Bob is going to sing that song someday at my wedding. He is. It's a fact. I know it."

Hope leaped forth once more. It was as though, through the song's magic, I was able to see down the avenue of years to a day when Bob would be set free from that prison he was in, free to sing this song at his sister's wedding.

I felt I had just been given a beautiful gift, not only a new record that would remind me of my lost son, but much more than that. I had been given the gift of hope. And I knew who the Giver was.

One Sunday morning, curious about the Evangelistic Temple, Tom decided we both should go. I had not expected this, knowing he preferred the quiet regulated ritual of an Episcopal service. Yet that morning as we sat there, caught up in circumstances we did not comprehend, propelled to a church outside our ken—we were open, vulnerable, expectant.

I kept glancing at Tom during the service, highlighted as it was with hearty gospel music and spontaneous prayers, trying to gauge his reaction. Unreadable. He would only pat my hand and smile reassuringly as if to say, "Don't worry, I'm not going to bolt."

There was an altar call that morning, when people were encouraged to come forward to the railing and accept Jesus as their Savior or rededicate their lives to Him. And an inner battle began in me.

As the pastor's voice called softly, "One more, there is one more," I recalled the skepticism I had always felt for such tactics. I tried to marshal the defenses I had built up through the years. All to no avail. Everything crumbled before the power of that Voice, the One who was truly calling me.

I turned to Tom.

"Darling, I'm sorry," I whispered. "I hope I don't embarrass you too much, but I have to go forward."

He leaned over and hugged me.

"Then go," he said, his voice husky.

As I walked slowly down the long aisle, I heard some words faintly familiar yet strange to my lips, coming quietly from the depths of me. Through a flood of tears, I murmured over and over: "O Lord, I believe. Help Thou my unbelief. O Lord, I believe. Help Thou my unbelief."

I was still praying softly when an elder knelt with me at the railing and spoke words that penetrated like a laser: "Yes, He will do that when you ask. He will draw out all unbelief and dispose of it. He is faithful."

A faint echo from a distant time.

Tom's diary later recorded it succinctly:

A.M. Evangelistic Temple with Frankie. She went up to the altar. A very moving experience.

Soon after, as if drawn by a magnet, I went back alone to an evening service. At one point the congregation was asked to say this sentence prayer: "O Lord, let me share Your burdens."

And we did so, repeating it again and again: "O Lord, let me share Your burdens."

I believe a breaking happened in many hearts that night. I know it did in mine. My focus shifted from me and my heartbreak over Bob, to others in the Children of God and to their parents, to those caught up in the dope and alcohol craze infecting our nation, to the families being torn apart by divorce, to those ill with cancer, disease, mental illness . . . and on and on.

Through the meaning of these words, as they began to cut through our human defenses, a corporate compassion welled up in that gathered body. We were taking our eyes off ourselves and our individual petty or real problems. In unison we spoke. In unison we heard. In unison we received the message.

"O Lord, let me share Your burdens." Such a simple phrase, spoken softly, in unity all over the huge room. Hundreds of voices, over and over . . . "O Lord, let me share Your burdens."

Breaking down barriers . . . cutting through to our hearts . . . feeling His pain for His beloved.

I wept. In my memory, we all wept. We wept as one. We wept as one with Him.

The One who wept over Jerusalem . . . And now mourns over His lost ones.

The Holy One of Israel.

13

This Thing Is from Me

The next day I came down with the flu. Always impatient with illness, I tried to ignore it and stayed in bed only a day. My fever returned, and I was forced back to bed. Once more I popped out, too soon. This time our doctor took a firm hand, suggesting I curtail my business activities and ordering bed rest and quiet until I had fully recovered. I was strangely relieved and slept soundly around the clock.

When at last I awakened, my eyes fell on my Bible and I reached out for it, almost hungrily. Mindful of my abortive attempts in the past, I decided to turn to something familiar. Everyone's all-time favorite seemed safe enough, so I opened to the Twenty-third Psalm.

"The Lord is my shepherd; I shall not want."

Such a simple declaration. So strengthening, if it were true.

"God, have I ever let You be my Shepherd? Have I ever really let You be my Lord?"

I suddenly saw myself during a period in Levittown after Kathy's healing when I had made a conscious effort to do just that. It had been almost a game—looking for God's guidance, even in little things.

101

"I remember a peace during that time," I prayed now. "I did know Your presence then. I even called You Lord, and I talked to You just like this. Remember? I asked You to help me drive to Garden City right after I got my driver's license and was petrified. And You did that, too. It all seemed so right and believable. Why did I stop talking to You and asking for Your help?"

My eyes went on to the next verse: "He maketh me to lie down in green pastures . . . ."

"You make me lie down!" I was startled. "This is Your doing—my lying here sick?"

He makes me to lie down. I had never seen that meaning before. "Are You really doing this?"

"He leadeth me beside the still waters. He restoreth my soul."

It was more peaceful to read His Book than to question Him. The old, familiar words performed their magic. I felt calmed and soothed. I pictured a still pool, with trees reflected in it and a distant mountain. The Smokies moved in close, and I felt their strength and protection enfolding me.

"I shall restore your soul." Softly, like a voice in the shadows.

I drifted off to sleep again, comforted like a little child safe in her father's arms. *I shall not want. I shall not want . . . .*

When Tom came in that evening, he handed me a typewritten sheet.

"A young girl in our office told me to give you this," he said with a teasing smile. "She heard you were sick. She says she's particularly interested in your case."

My curiosity was aroused. "My case? What does she mean?"

"Well, she's an interesting character, with a lingo all her own. I'm not sure what she means, exactly, but—"

Tom sat down, suddenly serious. "Her name is Lynne Argyries. She's a Greek girl, and a Christian. She mentioned witnessing in the park the other day. I asked if she had ever heard of the Children of God. She sure had. It seemed that she and her buddies from an Episcopal church downtown somewhere"—he nodded his head knowingly at my look of astonishment—"go as a team to witness in the park every weekend. She's especially interested in the Children of God bunch. She sees the real danger there. Says she gets a headache every time she 'raps' with them. For safety, she never talks to them alone. Their cause is the Children of God, she says, and not Jesus Christ."

"That's a wise observation," I remarked.

"Anyway, that day I told her about Bob, and she was obviously concerned. It's been good for me to have someone in the office to discuss it with once in a while. Well, today after I mentioned that you were sick, she came by just as I was leaving the office, and said something like, 'I'm on your wife's case. I know she's hurting. Tell her to read this when she feels like it.' Then she skipped on. I haven't read the paper myself."

Tom paused a moment, then added softly, "She's praying for us and for Bob."

I looked at the paper with real interest after Tom left the room. It said:

Found in J.N.D.'s Bible
(Translated from the French)

DISAPPOINTMENTS?

"This Thing Is from Me" (I Kings 12:24)
The disappointments of life are in reality only the decrees of love. I have a message for thee today. My child, I will whisper it softly in thine ear, in order that

the storm-clouds which appear may be gilt with glory, and that the thorns on which thou mayest have to walk be blunted. The message is but short—a tiny sentence—but allow it to sink into the depths of thine ear, and be to thee as a cushion on which to rest thy weary head: "This thing is from Me."

There was more, but for the moment my brimming eyes prevented my reading on. I felt overwhelmed. It's not every day when one asks the Almighty a question that one gets a prompt, personal reply, neatly typed and hand-delivered by one's own loving husband.

"And via some strange little Greek angel who's been 'put on my case,'" I mused. "Lord, You are too much!"

Smiling a little now, I continued to read. It was a long message, but certain parts seemed to be ringed with neon lights:

Hast thou never thought that all which concerns thee, concerns Me also? He that toucheth thee toucheth the apple of Mine eye. That is why I take a special interest in thine upbringing.

I let the phrases caress me. "Oh yes, I know love when I hear it." (Shades of my long-gone grandmother.) "How could I close my ears to One who wooed me with such tender words?"

Then these words caught my attention:

I am the God of circumstances. Thou hast not been placed where thou art by chance, but because it is the place I have chosen for thee.

That thought startled me. "Are You really that much in charge, God?" (Dangerous idea!)

Art thou passing through a night of affliction? "This thing is from Me." I am the Man of sorrows and acquainted with grief (Isaiah 53:3). I have left thee without human support, that in turning to Me thou mightest obtain eternal consolation (II Thessalonians 2:16-17).

I gazed beyond the paper for a moment.

"What I'm hearing," I prayed, "is that You are in charge! Would You—could You allow all this to happen, that I might truly turn to You? Do you really want me that much? Unworthy me?"

The surprising message continued:

Thou hast been laid on one side, on a bed of sickness and suffering. "This thing is from Me." I was unable to attract thine attention whilst thou wast so active. I wish to teach thee some of My deep lessons. It is only those who have learned to wait patiently who can serve Me.

Now there was the direct answer to my question asked earlier that day. I couldn't help but hear this!

"Forgive me, Lord," I prayed. "I have always been too busy. Thank You for making me listen. Keep me tuned in. I don't know if I can ever wait patiently."

Then another passage jumped out:

Hast thou made plans and then come, asking Me to bless them? I wish to make thy plans for thee. I will take the responsibility, for it is too heavy for thee; thou couldst not perform it alone (Exodus 18:18). Thou art but an instrument and not an agent.

"How You know me when You say that! I'm always asking You to bless *my* plans. I thought You wanted *my* initiative."

No, dear one. Let Me initiate. You are to respond.

So clear! I could hear that now so clearly. It was liberating, too, just calling my own creativity forth to its highest achievement, like a maestro drawing out the purest notes from his musicians.

There was more, but my eyes skipped down to where the message ended with these words:

> This day I place in thy hand a pot of holy oil. Draw from it freely, My child, that all the circumstances arising along the pathway, each word that gives thee pain, each manifestation of thy feebleness, may be anointed with this oil. Remember that interruptions are divine instructions. The sting will go in the measure in which thou seest Me in all things. Therefore set your heart unto all the words that I testify among you this day. For it is your life.
>
> (Deuteronomy 32:46-47)

For it is your life. For it is your life. Those last words lingered.

All the words were powerful, and most of them spoke to me right where I lived. Yes, this is my own life, to be lived once, right now! And my God is speaking to me. He has been for some time, but I have been too bullheaded to stop and listen. He has my attention now, in a new way, as He never has had before. And I feel as if He is really hearing me, too.

Emboldened, I continued in all honesty:

"Lord, I've always hated interruptions with a passion. Keep reminding me that interruptions are Your instructions. Help me—please help me, Lord—to see You in all things. Give me that sensitive awareness of You that will enable me to do that. And Lord, teach me about that pot of holy oil—that pot of oil You said I may draw on freely in all my circumstances. I don't understand that. But I trust You to teach me. I do want You to be my best friend. I want You for my confidant. Do You really long to be mine?"

The intense conversation seemed to be coming to a close. I felt myself unwinding, the most relaxed I had been in ages. Sleep, blessed sleep, like a wispy chiffon gown, was falling softly all around me. What peace tonight in this luxurious cocoon woven by my God, the God of circumstances. Even my dream was painted by His hand.

14

The Paint Pot

That night my ebbing thoughts blended into this series of dreams, which were vivid and deeply significant.

I find myself standing on the edge of one of nature's strange creations, the Paint Pot. It is an active boiling mass of grayish mud, bubbling and gurgling in restless, unending motion.

I recognize it from our visit to Yellowstone Park twelve years before. At that time I stood beside it transfixed, as I watched bubbles bulge up and pop, sending out ever-changing circles of pastel colors that mingled with other circles of delicate hue. Sulphuric fumes tainted the unearthly beauty of the place, making me wonder if it could be the devil's own brew. Yet the odor was not noxious enough to break the spell that gripped me.

Forgotten for years, the Paint Pot scene now looms in vivid color, framing my dream place, holding me once again spellbound.

The turbulence seems to subside into a gentle, undulating movement as I watch. I see one bubble rise and pop with a pleasant, clear sound. Instead of sulphur, I catch the fresh

fragrance of a spring day and am whirled back to my childhood as Miss Mamie, my grammar school teacher, comes into
view. Lean and tall, face tiny under all that hair, she is speaking plainly to me. Her eyes behind her glasses are magnified
and hold mine like a magnet.

"Listen carefully to all instructions, Fonde." (She always
called us by our last names.) "Then be obedient. Remember
obedience."

The tone is so familiar.

"Are you God?" my child-voice asks her.

Her face changes expression swiftly. The prim old-maid
visage that was her classroom mask is clearly startled, almost
angry. Then I see it melt into a warm, unlined young countenance with a beaming smile of pure love. But she does not
answer.

I see another bubble forming and growing, and hear a
champagne cork popping. As I watch the brightly colored
ripples fanning out, I realize that I am hidden in a secret place
under the swinging bridge at Camp Margaret Townsend with
Sally B. We are watching the mountain stream flow by. Insects
are humming in the soft summer air. A breeze moves the
leaves of the tree gently beside us as a branch bows to touch
the water.

"Darlin'," Sally B.'s voice whispers. "This is very important."

She is my beloved Scout leader and Sunday school teacher. I
adore her and always hang on every word. Now she is to
instruct me about confirmation. (Normally in the Episcopal
Church, one takes confirmation classes for several weeks at
around age 12. Mother has made special arrangements, however, in this my twelfth summer, for Sally B. to prepare me in
one session while at camp, so that I can be confirmed upon my

return home. It has been promised that I will take the formal classes later.)

Now I see that lovely moment recreated. I do not hear all of Sally B.'s words. Her voice is a soft murmur against the musical notes of the brook tumbling over the rocks.

A few words come through with pristine clarity: "The Holy Spirit is a Person. A real Person, darlin'—as real as you or I."

I look out across the stream through the leaves of the overhanging branch. It is a moment when all nature stops. Absolute quiet. No water murmurs. No bird calls. No insect whirrs. And I see a breeze, a gentle wind, coming across from the other shore. Soundlessly it stirs the branches, making dimpled ripples in the water. He comes through the leaves and touches me. I feel His breath on my face. I look at Sally B., my eyes wide with the wonder of it, and see that she too knows He is with us.

The scene is fading. I want to hold onto it.

Now I see another bubble rising in the framework of my dream. There's a choral backdrop, soft and unintelligible at first, but I soon make out the words: "And when you search for Me, and when you search for Me with all your heart . . . I will be found of you, I will be found of you."

I recognize the yearning, seeking, restless spirit that is at home in me—an old friend. I expect to see the friend take form and face when I hear the gentle swoosh of the bubble bursting. Instead, I am transported to the back porch of my youth in Morningside, where Dad and I are gazing at a blue-black sky radiant with stars.

I hear Dad explaining patiently something about the incredible distance between us and the moon, and between the moon and the stars, and on and on. I want to ask him to stop, but I do not dare.

It is too much to contain. It is overpowering me. I see Dad

getting bigger and bigger, nearly tall enough to touch those heavenly lights. But I feel myself shrinking, getting smaller and smaller until I am almost gone. Dad does not seem to notice and continues expounding on the vastness of space and the wonder of creation.

The smallness of me is awed by the greatness of the one beside me whose head is now out of sight. I feel myself slip through a crack in the floor, aware of the dark basement below like a black pit; and I am falling out of control, tumbling over and over toward it. A giant hand reaches down and catches me easily. I am as light as a feather. It holds me tenderly so as not to break me or even muss my dress. A protective love is all around me, and I feel cherished.

I keep my eyes closed. The moment is too precious for vision. Yet, childlike, I peek. For one fleeting instant I see a guardian thumb—strong, immense, but also soft and gentle, crooked high above me and the cradle of safety in which I rest. Quickly I close my eyes again and bask in the warmth of a mysterious tender mercy.

Oozing from one level of dream-state to another, I see that I am truly in the basement of our Morningside home. It has been transformed from the musty, dark place of my memory to one of shining cleanliness and beauty. Everything is bathed in a glorious light—intense, yet soft, not blinding.

I see an ornate box where Dad's large toolchest used to be. It draws me. As I come close I see that it is an elaborate casket. My son, Bob, is lying in it, seemingly asleep, peaceful and serene. The lining is made of a brilliant fuchsia satin. I feel dismay—not that Bob is in a casket, but because I know he will detest its extravagance and gaudiness.

"I need to find another for him before he comes to," I decide to myself. "A plain wooden box would be just right."

In the furnace room I locate a wooden chest, and somehow,

with the effortlessness that dreams allow, I get him transferred from one to the other. I feel relief when I see him in the
plain pine coffin lined with rough homespun cloth.

"There, that's much better," I sigh. Yet a sense of uneasiness
lets me know that there is still something amiss about the
situation.

My eye is caught by a sign hanging above Bob in the box. I
have been aware of it, but have not read it. It grows larger and
larger, and now I see: *The Living Dead*.

"The living dead, the living dead," I repeat aloud, slightly
perplexed, but not in the least horrified.

The sunny light seems to intensify. My being is still immersed in the knowledge that I am completely under the
protection of an all-encompassing Love and Wisdom. An
understanding dawns and with it comes joy.

"There's to be a resurrection! Of course, a resurrection!" I
whisper with gladness.

Another bubble swirls into view and with the sound of its
pop, I awake. In my bedroom the early morning sunlight
bathes me gently, pushing back the shadows in my room. A
lightness and contentment pervade me, as I experience a
peace I've never known before.

In that "between" state, where the dream world was releas-
ing its hold and the real world was beckoning, I began to
examine what had been said to me through the medium of the
Paint Pot.

The dream was one big awareness of God, I decided. The
message sent by the girl in Tom's office had deftly slashed a
large chink in my armor. And God's love had flowed through
and penetrated my unconscious. With the Paint Pot as His
palette, and using wide, easy paint strokes, the Master Artist

had recreated some scenes from my memory store. He had revived with fresh poignancy some almost-forgotten moments in my life when He had been real to me.

The Paint Pot at Yellowstone was like my life and everyone's life, all roiling and bubbling within, sending out pale circles of lovely colors and occasional whiffs of disturbing odors, yet holding a compelling fascination.

I remembered that there were dried-up, cracked places on the outskirts of that strange pond in the park, where there was evidence of past activity but that now looked dead and useless. And in some spots colors had become so mingled that there was ugliness rather than beauty. That, too, could correspond to our lives.

But the Paint Pot of my dreams—oh, *that* Paint Pot—had pure colors of rich, vivid hue, and emitted only fresh, clean aromas. Even the motion of it was gentle and controlled, as if under the power of Someone blessed with unlimited ability and all-seeing wisdom.

It seemed to me that each little vignette in my dream reminded me of a time in my life when I had allowed God to break through and make Himself known to me.

I had sensed Miss Mamie's love for us as she taught us important lessons in our formative years, even though she seemed stern and unyielding. Perhaps in my child-mind I had thought of her a bit as God, and had come out with a somewhat muddled view of Him in the process. I could see that, in my dream, those facets of her character that I had glimpsed as Him were pointed out and clarified to my inner satisfaction. I had actually learned some important things about Him through her, although she never had the slightest idea that I had. She never talked about God.

You were searching for Me, even then.

My heart gave a glad leap. I had not thought of it that way.

"And You revealed some of Yourself to me whenever I sought You," I marveled aloud in reply.

"That time with Sally B.," I reflected to the Lord, "tucked away in my memory cupboard, had gotten dusty and covered with cobwebs, till You washed it with freshness in my dream. That day with her was the first time You came to me so that I knew You. And there was another witness—Sally B. She knew."

Wherever two or three are gathered in my name . . . .

"Thank You for reviving that precious moment. I'll never forget it again. And thanks, too, for reclaiming that evening with Dad, and the stars, and the light years, and You."

That was a night I had thought of many times, a time not hidden away like the other. I had often recalled the awe that came over me as I explored the limitlessness of the universe with my earthly father, and had come to experience in the process my heavenly Father, the One who is larger than it all.

"How can I retain that sense of safety and rightness that I glimpsed that night long ago, and knew with surety in my dream, and am still savoring right now?"

Abide in me, and I in you. . . came swiftly into my consciousness—not as an impossible commandment, but as a loving encouragement.

"Thank You, Lord."

The One who makes all things new had surely been reminding me of His power to rejuvenate, starting with our dingy Morningside basement.

"If You can do that," I reasoned with a smile, "You can redo me. Yes, even me!"

Tom entered the room with my breakfast on a tray.

"I'm leaving for the office. Got to run. Now, stay there in

bed. We want you well this time." He was using his best "doctor" voice.

He stooped, kissed my forehead, then stepped back to see if I planned to heed his advice. I could see pleased surprise on his face.

"You look better!" he exclaimed.

"Yes," I said, and grinned. "I had the most marvelous dream!" I paused. "And I'll stay here till I'm well."

15

Listening

A pebble dropped into the still pond of my mind: *In returning and rest you shall be saved, in quietness and in confidence shall be your strength . . . .*

The words sank deep into my early morning "clear pool" and sent out a series of ever-widening circles. I had dozed off after Tom left. Then a bright day had greeted me as my eyes opened. Now came these words, dropped lightly into my fresh, undisturbed consciousness. I spoke them softly aloud, with a question in my voice.

"In returning and rest I shall be saved? In quietness and in confidence shall be my strength?"

I knew where those lines came from—my favorite prayer in *The Book of Common Prayer,* "The Prayer for Quiet Confidence."

"What are You saying to me, God?" It was getting easier to talk to Him.

There was silence. I slipped on my robe, went into the den and found my prayer book—and a pack of cigarettes, too. Then, since my legs still felt wobbly, I climbed back into bed.

Lighting a cigarette, I flipped open my little leatherbound

book to the exact page. That startled me. But I read the prayer out loud:

> *O God of peace, who has taught us that in returning and rest we shall be saved, in quietness and in confidence shall be our strength; By the might of thy Spirit lift us, we pray thee, to thy presence, where we may be still and know that thou art God; through Jesus Christ our Lord. Amen.*

I started to take a puff on my cigarette, but instead hastily put it out. One doesn't pray and smoke at the same time, I reasoned, especially when asking to come into the Almighty's presence!

"I'd like to be still and know that You are God, but I sure was looking forward to that cigarette. I feel deprived. Now, how's that for honesty, God?" I giggled, feeling exasperated nevertheless.

Silence again—but warm, comfortable silence.

"This is ridiculous, Sir. I hope You'll forgive me, but I am going to smoke in Your presence."

And I relit the same cigarette.

At ease, I began to read the prayer again as the smoke now curled around my head.

"O God of peace, who has taught us that in returning and rest . . . ."

"That sounds as if You've given us a lesson about returning and rest," I said. "When did You teach us about that?"

An echo of Sally B.'s voice sounded dimly in my mind: *At least three-fourths of the prayer book comes from the Bible.*

I had recently discovered a concordance in the back of my Bible. Now, on impulse, I looked up the word *confidence*. There it was: "In confidence shall be your strength"—Isaiah 30:15.

This is fun, I thought. *I'm on an adventure!*

My fingers turned the pages of my King James Bible rapidly.

Isaiah 30:15 read like this: "For thus saith the Lord God, the Holy One of Israel; In returning and rest shall ye be saved; in quietness and in confidence shall be your strength . . . ."

I was amazed. My favorite prayer came from the Bible, and the words from the Lord God Himself! "The Holy One of Israel," it said.

Then I remembered I had called Him by that name the other night at the Temple as we said the sentence prayer over and over. From somewhere had come those words, "The Holy One of Israel." I was awed, and the hairs on the back of my neck stood up.

"You are communicating with me!"

I sat there in bed with my hand over my mouth, my eyes wide. If He had chuckled out loud, I would not have been surprised.

Something nudged me to read on. There was a colon and four more words. But my heart sank as I read them. They were short, one-syllable words that pierced me: *"And ye would not."*

"No, I would not," I said to the Lord. "It's true. You've been showing me for some time that I do know about that *rest-in-You* place. I do know what You mean about returning and coming back to You. I've been there many times, but I always end up turning back to my own way.

"That day on the bank of the river," I continued, "under the swinging bridge when You breathed on me was so forgotten that it took Your dream to revive the memory. When the children had polio, I turned to You, but forgot Your mercy so quickly. When the doctor told us Kathy's bone growth was a miracle, I soon found a natural explanation for it. When I recognized You in my black pit of despair as the One to bring me out—the only One who could—I took full credit for my recovery. When I drove to Dallas to try to get Bob out, it was *my* way, with a bare acknowledgment of Your help."

My thoughts stumbled now over Bob. The sign in my dream came back to me: *The Living Dead*. Had I, in my everyday world, been mourning Bob as if he were truly dead? Yes. I could see I had been walking around in grief, thinking of him as gone.

"God, why? Why did You let this happen to him?" Anger stirred in me. "If You are a loving God—why?"

Trust in the Lord with all thine heart; and lean not unto thine own understanding. In all thy ways acknowledge him, and he shall direct thy paths.

My anger had evidently stirred up the memory of those verses in Proverbs, which had angered me months before. Tracing my anger back a bit, I recalled the cold fury that had taken control of me when Newman gave me "praise" verses instead of going to Mingus to sweep Bob out of there. Now I made an attempt to forget anger and to "return."

In returning and rest you shall be saved, I repeated quietly, several times. *In quietness and in confidence shall be your strength.*

"What are You showing me, Father? I want to learn from You. I need rest and quietness of soul. I want to trust You. But how do I go about it when Bob is with that weird group and I am sick to my very bones about it?"

My cigarette pack was half-empty by now. I felt a calm returning. My agitated "pond" was beginning to smooth out to gentle shimmering. What was it Miss Mamie had said? Something about listening.

"Listen carefully to all instructions, Fonde."

Then what?

"Then be obedient. Remember obedience."

I cringed at that despised word.

"I'll start with listening," I decided.

I knew I had never been a very good listener, too wrapped up in my own thoughts, more eager to be heard than to hear. So I knew I needed better listening qualities, whether listening to the Spirit or man.

But I suspected that in order to hear God, even more would be required: an extra ounce of awareness; longer, more sensitive antennae; greater yieldedness than merely being open; and enough flexibility to hear Him in ways other than audible words, or that whisper in my spirit.

Due to anguish over my son's predicament, I had been more open than ever before to hear God. In fact, I was surprised at the many ways I had been aware of His direct communication with me.

He had made Himself known to me through circumstances, through the Bible, through other written material (specifically, the paper sent to me as if on cue by my Greek "angel"), through my own dreams, through other people, through their actions or words (usually when they were totally unaware of it), and even through music.

I began to recall some of these experiences—moments when the light had dawned, when there was a breakthrough, when I knew it had been God. At those times, the most natural thing in the world had been to think, *Aha!* And I had been a-tingle with the "rightness" of the experience and awash with joy.

Now I found myself yearning to hear Him. Usually an "Aha!" experience happened when least expected, and I wondered if I could hear Him when I actively tried.

"I don't even know how to go about it," I murmured. "I'm a poor listener."

Be still and know that I am God. That part of the prayer I had been reading before began to hum through my mind. So I tried to do just that.

The phone rang. It was Newman. I told him I had been thinking about those praise Scriptures he had given me 'way back in June, and I asked him about praise.

Newman showed me a vivid word picture from Psalm 22:3—that God inhabits the praise of His people.

It was a new, faith-building thought. Also, Newman pointed out that something happens to us as we turn ourselves to God in true praise. Our own attitudes change and can affect our relationship with Him in a powerful, positive way.

I realized two things when I hung up the phone. First, I realized that God had prompted Newman to phone just then, at that moment.

Secondly, I realized that I had not misunderstood God the time I felt moved to call Newman before Susan's wedding. I simply had not been open to the message He had given me through His emissary—in part because I had expected something else.

Now, feebly, because I did not really know how, I began to praise my God.

That phone call from Newman was the beginning. From then on, through my days of convalescence, and as my heart was intent on trying to hear the Father, He spoke to me through His many voices: through His Holy Word; in quiet moments alone in my room; through phone contacts with Frances, Rose Marie, Charlsie, Newman and others; and through books, such as *Face Up with a Miracle*, by Don Basham, and *They Speak with Other Tongues*, by John Sherrill, both of which spoke to me about the baptism in the Holy Spirit, and *Beyond Ourselves*, by Catherine Marshall, which described a spiritual dimension of life that I could now relate to. Each day, brick by brick, a peace was built in me.

I heard the word *repent* a lot that week. It always conjured a picture in my mind of hand-painted words scrawled on rocks marring the landscape in eastern Tennessee: *Repent and Be Saved.* We used to see such desecrations of nature as we drove to the mountains. Daddy always snorted his indignation; and without my even realizing it, the word *repent* had become unacceptable in the process.

I decided to look it up in the dictionary. The first meaning given was "to turn from sin and dedicate oneself to the amendment of one's life." As simple and as complicated as that!

And ye would not. The words from Isaiah 30:15 took on a clear significance. Along with my new understanding of repentance grew a true longing to turn from myself as center of my world, to Jesus as Lord.

My cigarette habit became symbolic of my inability to turn from *me*, wholly and completely, and turn to Him. I had tried to stop smoking and could not. I felt a profound sadness at my human lack.

"I guess everyone has something that prevents such complete surrender," I said to the Lord. "For me it's cigarettes. For another it could be food, or liquor, or a husband, mother or child. Do I have another block, Lord? Have I ever—could I ever give You *Bob?*"

Bob? To stay in the Children of God? Oh, surely not that!

Once again seeking direction, I turned to Isaiah 30—this time in Tom's Bible, a Revised Standard Version. My eyes slid down the page to verses 19 and 20.

> *You shall weep no more. He will surely be gracious to you at the sound of your cry; when He hears it, He will answer you. And though the Lord give you the bread of adversity and the water of affliction, yet your Teacher will not hide Himself any more, but your eyes shall see your Teacher. And your ears shall*

hear a word behind you, saying, "This is the way; walk in it,"
when you turn to the right or when you turn to the left.

These words began a deep healing in me.

15

My Upper Room

FREECOG was holding an important meeting the next evening, and I felt well enough to attend with Tom. The Agape Force leaders had been consulted about the possibility of assimilating into their fellowship any Children of God members who might decide to leave the cult. Besides this report, some parents wanted to describe their latest experiences with COG.

After regular business, the meeting began on a good note with a favorable report on the Agape Force consultation. Their leaders were willing to interview any ex-COG members who were interested in joining them. They would do the same for anyone who wanted to be part of their group. (Screening was necessary since their group required demanding discipleship training and a full-time commitment.)

They were skeptical, however, that anyone from COG would be interested in them. Their earlier COG contacts revealed the members and even non-members as being so indoctrinated against groups connected even remotely with a church that they were scornful rather than eager to join.

The Agape Force also encouraged applicants to finish high

school and to have everything in order with their parents before making such a life-changing step.

This, too, clashed with COG doctrine. The Children were told to have nothing to do with "establishment" schools and were taught to hate their parents who had "let them down by not giving a true picture of God." Even those who had come out of COG were so warped in their thinking that many of these ideas clung to them tenaciously, and they had no desire to be candidates for the Agape Force. Still, the Agape Force was willing to try

The stark contrast between the methods of these two groups cast a cloak of gloom over everyone. I had not realized that when kids came out of "the cult," they would be so infected with COG thinking that they would carry doctrinal garbage with them. Perhaps those parents who believed the Children were being brainwashed had a point, though I had never seen any clear evidence of it.

In any case, the meeting moved from gloom into darkness—so dark, in fact, that most of it has been obliterated from my memory. I know several parents spoke, each telling a worse story than the one before. The evening wore on, with David Berg's role as chief villain being painted blacker and blacker. As parents reported their stories of hurt, the listeners sent out waves of empathy and everyone began to absorb the pain.

This was the only FREECOG meeting I ever attended that lived up to my worst fears of how a parents' group might behave. I don't know why this particular evening took that tone. But I was deeply affected by it. The weight of hate is heavy; and Tom and I walked out carrying a load of it.

Tom went right to bed, but I couldn't sleep. I went into our study, closed the door behind me, and started to sit down to read. Instead, I found myself putting the Bible on the chair seat, then sinking to my knees.

I had not yet turned on the reading light. The only light came from a dim lamp near the desk, and it filled the small room with a soft glow that barely illuminated the moss-green paneled walls. I could almost believe I was in a secret leafy bower hidden away high in the Smokies. There was an air of peace and serenity. In an instant this place had become a holy chapel for me, an "upper room."

Be still and know that I am God.

It was easy to do that in the quiet calm. I had found my resting place in Him. He welcomed me and I made myself at home.

I had no sensation of the passing of time. I seemed to be in a timeless sphere, where yesterday and tomorrow melded with the now.

Your Teacher will not hide Himself any more, but your eyes shall see your Teacher. And your ears shall hear a word behind you, saying, "This is the way; walk in it."

Blinders were gently removed from my spiritual eyes and cotton from my inner ears.

I will be found of you. Your eyes shall see your Teacher.

Promises kept. He was found and I could see. Love was visible, seen with my new eyes and heard with my new ears. The air was filled with light and faint music . . . and I *believed*.

The contrast between this atmosphere of love and peace, and the atmosphere so recently left behind, permeated by hate and confusion, brought me a strange new sensation. I was overwhelmed with compassion for the object of FREE-COG's hatred—David Berg. I don't pretend to understand it, but I was filled with a love and knowledge of David Berg that could not have come from myself.

Words began to fall softly from my lips. I was praying,

though I did not know how to pray. I cannot remember the exact words, but I do remember the general trend. I have ever since called it "my prayer of faith." But even the faith was not from me. It, too, was given to me as a gift. Only because I spoke it with my voice can I call it "my prayer."

The prayer began with words of compassion for the one I had been seeing as the Pied Piper of the Children of God. I saw him now as a man who had at one time been a true man of God, with his heart given to the Father. I saw him allowing some impediments within himself—perhaps pride and anger—to deceive him into taking the wrong path. The evil one who rules that path soon had him in tow. Bound in chains he did not see, and guided by forces he didn't realize controlled him, David Berg was leading others astray, including my own son.

I asked almighty God to open David Berg's eyes to his real predicament, and by His might free him from the bondage. I wept tears of pity and compassion for one I had been despising.

O Lord, let me share Your burdens.

My prayer turned to my son, also in bondage. It was a most specific prayer. I remember it a little better; perhaps this part was really my own.

"Lord God, I know it isn't Your perfect will for Bob to be in the Children of God. Therefore I will not clutter up this prayer with an 'If it be thy will' clause."

I felt a joyful release within me when I spoke these words. They were honest, and I knew He understood. I did not intend to weaken this prayer with any qualifiers. Don Basham's book had shown me that ours is a God of infinite power and might and had given me the confidence to pray with a new kind of boldness.

"Lord, I know You can do miracles today as when You

walked this earth. And I'm asking You to do one now. Not because I'm worthy—for I am not, and neither is Bob. But because it is right and within Your will, and because You have the power to do it.

"God—Father, Son and Holy Spirit"—I did not want to leave out any aspect of Him—"please do a miracle and bring Bob out of there in one month."

I caught my breath at the audacity of what I had just said. One month! That was really being specific! I heard myself beginning to laugh out loud, in His presence.

Then, stifling the laughter: "I know You could do it in one day, but I'll give You a month."

That didn't sound right, so I amended it hastily.

"I mean, I'm asking You to do it in a month." And I started to giggle again.

Then I stopped. Remembering the "sickness" of those who had come out of COG, I continued to ask God for more.

"And please make Bob whole after his release—whole enough to help others come out."

There, that was it.

"Amen. Oh yes, Father, in Jesus' name, Amen."

The prayer had ended. I felt a tremendous relief.

How can I express what happened next? It was a real miracle. It happened in an instant. *I knew!* I knew it was done: Bob was coming home. In God's eyes it was already done. Done! My prayer had been answered on the spot. And I had an absolute knowledge of it, as if it had already happened.

It was an "Aha!" experience *par excellence*.

I began to thank God and cry at the same time. I heard myself crying, "Oh, thank You," over and over, until a song of praise welled up in me and spilled out, overtaking the inadequate *thank You's*. The praise was sung by one who cannot sing, with words she did not understand. And it went on and on, till joyful praise filled every nook and cranny in the room and every fiber of the one who praised. Praise for the One who is worthy of praise.

Then I began to sing a song I had learned at the Evangelistic Temple: "Thou art worthy, Thou art worthy . . . ." As the last notes died away, I found myself quietly speaking to Him once more. For some reason, I was remembering a story from Sunday school days about Shadrach, Meshach and Abednego. With sudden insight, I grasped the parallel and my words flowed with real conviction:

"Now I see why those three have popped into my mind. Right before they went into the fiery furnace, they said something like, 'Our God will deliver us. But even if He does not, we will not worship your false gods, because ours is the one true God!' I feel the same way now, Lord, and I praise You.

"Father, I know You are going to bring Bob home—within the month. But even if You don't, You are my God. You are sovereign in this universe. And that's what I have come to realize as never before. And that is why I am praising You. Not because You answered my prayer, but because You are who You say You are! And I can trust any of my loved ones to You, into a fiery furnace, or into the Children of God. Bob is Yours, not mine. And I take my hands away from him. I give him to You."

Quietness fell over the room. His presence, fresh, new like a spring day, and brushed with light good humor, surrounded and upheld me.

The hand in my dream, I thought. *I am in the palm of His hand.*

I wanted to awaken Tom to tell him that Bob was coming home. But it was nearly dawn, and I knew he needed the sleep.

When the alarm went off, though, I told him right away.

"Honey, Bob is coming home," I said, joy breaking through at the knowledge of it.

Tom's face lighted up immediately. "When did he call? Last night? Why didn't you wake me?"

I had not planned this at all. I started picking my words with care.

"No, he didn't call. But, well—I went into the study . . . and Tom, I prayed. But it wasn't an ordinary, run-of-the-mill prayer. Oh, honey—" and it all came out in a rush.

"I asked God to bring Bob home in a month, and He said He would." I was watching Tom closely, and saw an odd expression cross his face.

"Don't doubt," I said earnestly, my eyes glued to his. "Please, honey, do not doubt. It's very important that you not doubt this. It's true."

"Darling," he replied with a slight grin, "I don't doubt it at all. But I was just thinking, how like my Frankie to give God a deadline!"

We burst into helpless laughter together. All the laughter I had stifled last night came out. Gales of laughter—the first real laughter in our house since Bob left last spring. Perhaps it was holy laughter. It was a magnificently freeing thing. We laughed in each other's arms until we cried.

Bob is coming home, I thought, *and now we both know it. Praise God!*

"My cup runneth over with joy," I hummed as Tom dressed.

"Tom, there's one more thing."

"Yes?" He braced himself.

"I'm afraid you're married to a 'holy roller.' "

"Oh, that," he said and kissed me. "I've suspected it all along!"

His diary for Tuesday, November 16, 1971, put it this way:

FREECOG meeting. F. had a Visitor.

17

God's Chosen Fast

Having been awake almost all night, I thought I should sleep. But I couldn't. I wasn't sleepy. I thought I should eat breakfast. But I couldn't. I wasn't hungry. In fact, food seemed superfluous. I was being fed with joy.

A reverent awe of all He had done and was yet to do placed me on the edge of high expectancy. From that vantage point, I had no need, at least for the moment, to minister to my body.

Perhaps I should fast, I thought fleetingly. I longed to do something for God to express my adoration, some outward act to show my devotion.

To me fasting, although I had had but slight exposure to it, had always reeked of asceticism. A religious discipline of self-denial, suggested for Lent and a few other times on the Episcopal calendar, fasting had not been emphasized in my church experience. Whenever it was, it had seemed a bit much.

The few times I had tried to follow the requirement, I had felt terribly self-righteous about it. If I managed to keep quiet about it, I went around with a secret judgmental scorn of those who were eating ("the gluttons"). Mostly, however, I tended to hint here and there, with a brave smile, about my self-deprivation, and ended up with a full-blown case of pride. Obviously I had never had any good teaching on the subject.

Since I could not understand what had caused me to think of fasting, I dismissed the idea immediately.

When I called Frances to share the good news of my "upper room" experience, she rejoiced with me about it, believed with me that my prayer was answered and that Bob would soon return; and then, with some hesitation, she suggested that the Lord might call me to fast.

Nothing she could have said would have surprised me more.

"Why," I stumbled, "that thought occurred to me only moments before I called you!"

"Good," she said, relief in her voice. "I wanted to be sure before I mentioned it that you wouldn't start to fast just because I suggested it, but only if the Lord calls you to it. To me, the fact you've already thought of it indicates He has already planted a seed. If He wants you to fast, there will be another confirmation—at least one, maybe more, but one for sure."

I was amazed. Even as she spoke the words, I realized that I was being given a lesson about God's guidance. I was hungry for more.

"The Lord never pushes," went on my Teacher, disguised as Frances, "but He gives His suggestions clearly, and usually more than once. When you're alert to Him, listening for His voice, you know. The third time for sure. The first time the seed is planted; the second time is like a watering; and the third time calls for faith action. What has been planted is ready to emerge.

"Of course, we could stand on the little green shoots and keep new life from happening, either through ignorance or stubbornness. But—" she paused for a moment and added, a smile in her voice, "an old-fashioned word like *obedience* comes to mind."

My amazement grew. *Listen and be obedient,* shades of Miss Mamie! I felt like a child in kindergarten with a good teacher. My awe at the Lord's ability to speak to me increased. I longed now to start a fast.

"I've got the picture, Frances! But do I have to wait for another sign? And tell me all you know about how to go about fasting. I don't know much about it, and what I do know seems all wrong."

Frances, taking her responsibility to me, the neophyte, launched earnestly into a fascinating teaching about fasting. She showed me how this ancient discipline is rooted firmly in the Scriptures. I well remember two points she made. One was that often the main purpose of a fast does not become clear until after it has ended. The other was that when God calls us to a fast, we should not set any limits on the time of it. He will show us when to end it, as well as when to begin it— and usually not in advance.

She was careful to give me principle and not law about God's guidance in this and other things.

"A third mention is likely—not a certainty, Frankie," she reminded me. "I call it *confirmation* of the thing in question. But you will know. He will confirm it in your heart. Maybe He's already done that in you this time, but I hope He'll confirm it some other way, graphically, so you'll understand more completely what I'm talking about."

Her parting suggestion was for me to go about my regular activities, not dwelling on it; and probably when I least expected it, in some way, I would *know* to fast.

That sounded like adventure to me! I was intrigued, and determined to try to follow her guidelines.

Taking her advice, I went about my housewifely chores that

morning. A lot had piled up during my illness. As I dusted and vacuumed, I sang and whistled and even felt like dancing. The effervescent joy within kept spilling out; and my mind began to roam over the past few months, savoring every moment that had contributed to establishing this new, very real relationship with the Lord.

He calls us out of darkness into His wonderful light.

A phrase I had heard at the Temple (probably a Bible quotation, I surmised) surfaced unexpectedly. I could picture it: darkness, the oppressive blackness of the FREECOG meeting, followed by Light, the springlike freshness and illumination that came into my study-chapel the night before. The Master Artist, ever at work, had created an exquisite miniature—an evening of drastic extremes that illustrated the reality of those words, *Out of darkness into His wonderful Light.*

How had it begun—this sense of communion, this recognition of a relationship?

I believe, Lord; help Thou my unbelief.

Was it that day I walked down the aisle at the Temple? Was that, for me, a necessary step toward real commitment? And from what hidden vault had those words come? I knew they were not my own words. I had been quoting something, someone. But what? Who?

Putting aside my cleaning for a moment, I turned again to my Bible concordance, my detective instinct at work.

There it was! Mark 9:24—"Help thou mine unbelief." The thrill of discovering buried treasure! I found that a man grieving for his son had said it to Jesus. I wondered what long-ago Sunday school teacher had read me those words and embedded them so deeply into my unconscious that I, another parent grieving for a son, had known to cry them out to Him, too.

I read the full story. The man had an ill son, whom he had

asked the disciples to cure, but they could not. The boy was afflicted with a "dumb spirit" that they were unable to cast out. When Jesus saw all the commotion, He asked what was going on, and the man stepped forward with his problem.

> *Jesus said unto him, If thou canst believe, all things are possible to him that believeth. And straightway the father of the child cried out, and said with tears, Lord, I believe; help thou mine unbelief.*

Tears, no less! Jesus rebuked the foul spirit, which left the boy. Then the King James Version puts it this way:

> *And he was as one dead; insomuch that many said, He is dead. But Jesus took him by the hand, and lifted him up; and he arose. And when He was come into the house, his disciples asked him privately, Why could not we cast him out? And he said unto them, This kind can come forth by nothing, but by prayer and fasting.*

Fasting! I nearly dropped the Bible. Here was the confirmation I had been looking for, just like that!

When I had spoken these words in the Temple, I had been aching for my son's deliverance—also from a wrong spirit, or at least from a group with a wrong spirit. And I, too, had wept.

The parallels stunned me. I could see even more correlation. The sign in my dream had shown me Bob as "The Living Dead." This boy, too, had appeared dead. But Jesus, by His own hand, had lifted him up.

Altogether, it was an "Aha!" of the first order.

"Lord, You don't have to speak to me out loud. You're doing it well enough in other ways!"

The Master Artist was also the Master Weaver, weaving the tapestry of my life without ever a loose strand. Whenever there appeared to be one thread hanging loose somewhere from months before, He would slip it deftly into His work of art at just the right moment, clarifying even more the emerging picture. This was a prime example.

Why had it taken me so long to see it? Why had I been so reluctant to trust God? How could I doubt that He had a plan for my life?

It was no hard test of obedience. With joyful anticipation, I entered into God's chosen fast. Perhaps all obedience should have this quality. My past obedience seldom had.

Strangely, I felt no need for food. Feeling deprived or hungry was evidently not the point of fasting. It seemed as if another kind of hunger assailed me: a desire to learn more about Jesus Christ, His words and what they meant for my life, right then, for that day, for that moment.

I also experienced a greater desire to be with those who had had a personal encounter with Him. The fast served to keep me close to my Teacher, eager to hear His voice and ready to follow His lead. It helped me to take my eyes off myself and an "experience," and focus them on the One to whom I had given up my "throne." In no way did I fast for a reward, yet the rewards were many.

I developed a huge appetite for Bible study and was led (with confirmation as described by Frances) to my first real Bible class in a nearby neighborhood with women, seekers like myself, from many denominations. Janie, our teacher, who claimed to be no expert, was just right for us. She had an intimate relationship with the Inspirer of the Bible, as well as a wealth of knowledge about what was in His Book.

My Bible teaching up to that point had been from a critical, intellectual viewpoint that examined the Bible as though it

were an archaeological tomb, musty with age and slightly
suspect. This scholarly technique never advanced my Christian growth. In fact, it dampened any desire I might have had
to read those pages.

Being taught by this academic method was a little like being
forced to learn all the machinery of an airplane's engine—how
it worked, who had manufactured this part, why this part
could be considered obsolete—when all I really wanted was to
learn how to fly.

Janie's true gift was to teach us to fly. She taught us how to
read, study and inwardly digest God's holy Word. We learned
how to apply it to our everyday lives. We learned to stand
expectantly, wherever we were, till the wind of His Spirit blew
out of those pages and lifted our earthbound selves into the
air, and we were set free to soar.

Another aspect of the fast was the blossoming awareness of
how God was truly involved in the minute details of my life.
Each day seemed to bring some new revelation of His loving,
tender care to which before I had been blind. It was an ex-
panding, stretching, growing time.

I clutched the mystery of my fast to myself as a precious
secret, sharing it with no one. It was too holy, too private to
put into words.

When it ended several days later (with clear direction, as
Frances had predicted), I made such an unexpected discovery
at the last moment that I was awed.

My secret fast over, Tom and I were going out. I was checking my purse that evening to make sure I had everything I
needed, yet I kept feeling something was missing. Finally it
came to me—my cigarettes.

My cigarettes! I had not smoked a cigarette since the smoke-
filled FREECOG meeting four days before. And not once
during the fast had I thought of a cigarette. Not once! The

thought of a cigarette, in fact, now made me sick. My desire to smoke was eradicated. Gone. I had not licked my habit; I had not even prayed for deliverance from it.

Rather, it had become part of the miracle: God had simply taken it away.

18

"Feelings"—from A to Z and Back Again

That whole week following my faith prayer, I greeted each day with growing incredulity. This joy, this lightness of spirit, this feeling of rightness did not go away. It began to assume a lasting quality. Could it really be?

I was half-afraid it might evaporate like some misty dream that you want to hold onto but cannot. Since I was accustomed to early morning gloom—a faint sense of foreboding that had awakened me almost daily for years—this new pleasure was heady tonic.

Darker gloom had come with the Children of God, starting with a vague unease that had mushroomed into full-fledged dread. I had known some mornings of relief, when I had learned to cope with this heavy spirit enough to pull myself up by my bootstraps and not let it cling all day. But it took effort—lots of it.

Now I had burst out of the dark tunnel into daylight. I was basking in soft, balmy air. Instead of a leaden "What do I have to do today?", it became the joyful anticipation of "What do we do today, Lord?" Each day—a new adventure!

One evening Tom and I had plans to see a play with two other couples, the Mills and the Moodys, who were good friends. Since the night of my faith prayer nearly a week before, I had been looking forward to sharing with them all the amazing revelations I had been receiving. I anticipated that they would know by my glowing countenance (which even I could see was different) that "something has happened to Frankie."

So I could scarcely wait for my opportunity to expound on all that had taken place. I could imagine their delight as I told "my story," and expected they would receive with belief, just as Tom and Frances had, the news of Bob's imminent return. After all, our dearest friends should certainly be let in on this fantastic event.

The night before our theatre date, I began a mental rehearsal of my little speech. I hardly knew where to begin. They knew nothing of my trips to the Evangelistic Temple, or of Frances, or of the baptism in the Holy Spirit. We had not even dwelled much on our experience with COG and FREECOG, and our growing horror at Bob's predicament.

I began to realize that, though these two couples were indeed our good friends, we had all been adept at keeping our relationship on a fairly superficial level.

To be sure, we had a deeper bond with these four than we did with others, because we had cultivated one another's friendship. We had shared more deeply with them, and they with us, than is normally the case in our circle. Yet I wondered if our kinship was deep enough. How much could I say to them now? What would they accept? I wanted to be more than a visible witness to them; I wanted to tell them about my changed life.

But I began to feel very hesitant, and fell asleep with a sense of uncertainty.

The next morning I was greeted with that old familiar dead

feeling, and couldn't seem to shake it. I groped about for a reunion with the joy I had come so quickly to expect, but to no avail. I couldn't seem to recapture anything—a mood, a feeling, a place—that would restore me to that right relationship. What had gone wrong?

I tried to surmise, even as I tried to hide my distress from Tom, what the cause of this malaise could be. Perhaps it was Bob's refusal to go with us to Tennessee to celebrate my parents' upcoming golden wedding anniversary. We had expected this, but still it had hurt. Everyone in the family was coming, except Bob and one other grandson who had a valid reason. Discussing our plans for this trip helped me conceal from Tom and Kathy, who was home on vacation from school, how much I was hurting.

But by that night I had sunk into gloom. It was all I could do to look animated while our friends were chatting.

I hated the play. It was weird and unreal. Everything seemed askew. I was grateful only for the dark of the theatre.

Lord, You sure know how to humble a guy, I thought, hoping to establish contact with Him once more. *This was to be such a great evening, with me having my big chance to tell them all about You.*

I felt betrayed, yet I could hear "pride" in my plan for the evening; and even in the old, familiar idea of *my* plan.

At intermission each of our friends asked me privately, and ever so kindly, if I felt sick. My humiliation was complete. I could hardly speak for fear of bursting into tears. Had the faith prayer of a week before been a figment of my own fertile imagination? Where had my new life gone?

When they dropped Tom and me off at our door, I made a dash for the bedroom, whipped out of my clothes and into my nightie, jumped into bed, pulled the covers over my head and sobbed. To have been so high, and to have come so low, so fast: how could I ever trust anything again?

"Frankie, come here." My husband's voice sounded from somewhere in the house.

I ignored him.

Louder now. "Frankie, where are you? Come here, right now!"

Oh, be quiet, I muttered, but not out loud.

"Frankie, come here!"

There was something in Tom's voice that I couldn't decipher, something that puzzled me. He did not sound as though the house were on fire, yet there was a compelling urgency in his voice.

I went.

He was in the kitchen, his face strange. My heart began to pound. When I reached him, he took me gently by the shoulders and propelled me slowly around until my eyes were level with a note thumbtacked onto a cabinet above the counter.

In Kathy's handwriting, in large red letters, I read:

> *GOOD NEWS!!! Praise God! Praise God! Bob is coming home! He called tonight and will call again later to explain—but he is coming home! Praise God!*
>
> *Kathy*

I would like to think that I knelt down right then and there on the kitchen floor and asked for forgiveness for my faithlessness. But I don't think I did. All I remember is that Tom and I wept tears of joy together and danced around the room.

Here is Tom's diary report:

> *Theatre with Mills and Moodys. Bob called to say he was coming home.*

19

The Homecoming

Bob did call later that night to say he would come home Tuesday by thumb, bus or plane. He would need our financial help únless he hitchhiked. Tom said he would arrange plane-fare.

Bob sounded clipped and businesslike, his voice flat and lifeless. It was hard to stifle all our questions, but his manner held us at arm's length.

"I'll be able to go to the golden anniversary with you," he volunteered finally, right at the end. "They gave us our choice, Thanksgiving or Christmas, and I took Thanksgiving because of the anniversary. Others need the phone now. See you Tuesday."

We had to be content with that for the moment. We could not imagine what had happened to allow such a momentous change in policy. Speculation led us nowhere. I saw God's hand in it and decided to take the advice that had so bothered me before: *Lean not unto thine own understanding.*

Later, FREECOG learned the facts about this strange ex-odus: A wealthy man, taken in by their procuring tactics, had offered COG money and the use of a building as one of their schools, on the condition that those Children who so desired be allowed to visit their homes for either Thanksgiving or Christmas.

It had not been an easy decision for COG leadership to make, but after all-night sessions and several phone conferences with "Mo," they decided to accept. They expected to lose some of their converts in the process, but figured those kids to be expendable—dead wood, so to speak.

All of us in FREECOG were elated when we surmised that our newspaper publicity about the prisonlike qualities of the cult had been responsible for this benefactor's making such a requirement. If our publicity accomplished anyone's release, even in a roundabout way, we felt we were being effective.

After we talked to Bob on the phone that night, Tom went to sleep, but I found myself reflecting on my own strange ups and downs. How could I have gone from total belief to unbelief and back to belief so quickly? I felt ashamed, and asked for forgiveness.

The story of Peter—the one supposed to be the rock—and his denial came floating into my thoughts. I was comforted by the humanness of the apostle. I was always touched by Jesus' love for Peter whenever I read those passages. Jesus knew Peter through and through. He knew, even before Peter did, that Peter would deny Him, not just once but three times. Yet Jesus still loved Peter.

He loved *me* that way, too. I was forgiven.

Sleep came.

I called Frances first thing the next morning with the good news. Her voice bubbled with laughter.

"You gave God a month, you knew it could be done in a day, and He chuckled and did it in a week." That was Frances' immediate evaluation. And we laughed together. Frances also agreed to go with me to the airport to pick up Bob, since Tom could not get away.

Frances and I have since shared our recollections of the Tuesday we met Bob at the airport. Strangely, neither one of us can remember much about it. In general, we remember mostly his eyes—the glazed, staring, glassy look of one who is lost, afraid and without hope.

Frances had not seen him for more than eight months. Although I had tried to describe this peculiar look that I had seen from time to time, she was unprepared. Earlier that day we had prayed for God's understanding and wisdom to guide us. When she saw him, she knew we would need to rely on God entirely; that no human cleverness or wit could ever get through to him.

In fact, she confessed to me recently that as we drove back into town that Tuesday with Bob between us in the front seat, she came as close as she ever had since her conversion to doubting God's ability to make someone whole. Bob seemed totally out-of-reach, by either man or God.

With a mother's eye, I saw a lost waif wearing pathetic hand-me-downs, but clothed more tellingly in confusion and fear. He seemed cornered.

It was not easy to control my motherly instincts, which longed to wrap this "orphan chile" in a warm blanket of love. But I knew he would duck and run, and perhaps be irretrievably lost if any of us went too fast, too soon. This was going to take more delicacy than I possessed. It pushed me into God-dependence.

The thought of a psychiatrist crossed my mind, but I quickly dismissed it. I knew Bob would bolt at such a suggestion. Yet it was obvious Bob needed help—more help than we could give. We had to turn to God.

On the trip home from the airport we must have spoken. But neither Frances nor I can remember one word of conversation after we saw Bob.

Just eyes. We remember eyes—wide-open, unfocused, nonseeing. Eyes that did not respond. Unfathomable eyes that suggested a deep, dark well with fear at the bottom. They were dead eyes, the eyes of the living dead.

The living dead. With the memory of that odd dream being revived came also the glad thought that accompanied that dream: there was to be a resurrection. Of course, a resurrection!

He is faithful.

And another thought flashed: *God has brought Bob home one week from the day I prayed, instead of one month. He will make Bob whole, too. Some miracles just take longer than others.*

Hope was once again rekindled, and with it my own determination to take my hands off and start trusting God. To let Him do it!

Tom and I discussed privately our general plan of action—or rather, non-action—before embarking on our trip to Tennessee for my parents' golden anniversary. He agreed with me that we needed to "let go and let God"—that handy cliche we often heard bandied about in Christian study groups, with no one ever explaining quite how one did that. We didn't know how to either, but we resolved to try.

Since prayer had become talking frankly to a personal God, with real honesty, and then listening with new ears that could hear Him, I felt it was possible. The knowledge that I had a budding relationship with the One who is Love gave me confidence. And believing that He knew how to handle this situation, while we did not know how to at all, made it more natural to really trust Him.

Still, it was easier for Tom than for me. I had many bad habits to discard. When one has been trying to run the show for years, either behind the scenes or openly with abandon, it is not easy to put down the reins.

Tom felt that by treating Bob with love and concern in a natural, not oversolicitous way, the time would come when he would listen to us. We needed to demonstrate love for him but not for what he was doing. Tom also felt that when the time was right (and I felt the Lord would make this clear to us), we should tell him about our participation in FREECOG and show him the hard facts we had accumulated. Tom believed Bob would then decide of his own free will not to go back.

We concluded that one way we could show our love to Bob was by really listening to him with patience and interest. This would involve being uncritical and nonjudgmental, while at the same time maintaining our own integrity. We did not have to agree with what he was saying, but we should not put him on the defensive by disagreeing, at least until we had gained his confidence.

With all this in mind, we packed the car, slipping our FREE-COG information into the trunk along with our luggage, and set off early one morning for Tennessee.

I sat in the back with Bob so that he could give me a Bible lesson. It was not hard to feign interest, but it was hard to appear to be receiving the doctrine he was espousing without question. The lesson, once again, was about the end times, and involved an intricate timetable with numbers and dates making it appear as though the Children of God had an inside track as to the time of the Messiah's return.

When Bob asked if I believed his teaching, I postponed my answer by replying that I needed time to do some studying and evaluating before making a judgment.

This set the tone for the trip, and Kathy followed our example without being told. She had such an abiding love for Bob that it came easy for her. We were grateful for her wisdom and sensitivity. At one rest stop, she told me privately that Bob seemed to be two people, one a complete stranger and the other someone who resembled her brother only faintly.

This observation, perceptive in one so young, I heard echoed and reechoed as Tom and I compared notes later with other FREECOG parents whose sons or daughters came home for the holidays.

This "stranger" refused to eat with us in one restaurant when we stopped, sitting there silently with scornful disapproval. At another, he ate sparingly. Then, finishing before we did, he opened his Bible and began to read psalms in a loud, singsong voice for the benefit of all. It was hard to ignore, but we did.

In midafternoon Knoxville came into view, with the faint outline of the Smokies etched lightly in purple shadowing the background. I was home again.

20

Letting Go

The gathering of the clan in Knoxville was a joyous, bois-
terous, exciting occasion. Becki, Max and Lisa from Michigan
and Susan and Andy from Ohio were there when we arrived.
My three sisters and brother and all their spouses and children came—some 35 people altogether. My sister Anne and
her husband, Calvin, had just purchased a large lovely home
they had not moved into yet, which was being used as headquarters for all the festivities.

Tom and I were given the master suite; and we felt a bit like
the Beverly Hillbillies in the massive room with adjoining
marble bath. We were relieved to hear that Bob was to stay at
Mother and Dad's modest little place nearby, knowing he
would feel more at home there.

My family, an outgoing, affectionate bunch, had kept in
contact through the years. The uncles, aunts and cousins, not
to mention my proud mother and father, were delighted to be
seeing each other, as there had been no actual reunion since
1962.

Tom and I decided not to go out of our way to explain Bob's
situation to anyone unless asked. And everyone did ask,

privately, concerned by the obvious change in him. Each time we explained briefly about the Children of God and our hopes that he would decide not to go back. We told them we were counting on their love for Bob to help sway him.

My sister Alice's husband, Garnett, a tender man who loves kids, was especially solicitous. He came to us baffled by Bob's strange manner, feeling he could not get through to him. We could say only that we understood his bewilderment.

I could see Bob was doing his best, to no avail, to convert his cousins to the Children of God. As I walked near a table where he and some of his male cousins were chatting, I heard one of them remark, "What I hear you saying, Bob, is that you can't hack it in this society."

I hurried on, knowing what his answer would be: "I don't like this society and have no desire to hack it."

Another time, when Bob was strumming a borrowed guitar, his younger cousin Chuck joined him. From where they were sitting in the yard, they had a good view of the lovely old home that their uncle had so recently acquired—the one Tom and I were staying in. It had been built some 25 years before by a marble baron, and was lined not only with marble halls, but marble floors and bathrooms as well.

Chuck commented on the massive beauty of the place, which resembled a Spanish hacienda around a courtyard. Bob responded with some biblical reference to the transitory nature of material things, adding that all of it was nothing but dust.

"Yes," said Chuck, "but it's such a nice arrangement of dust."

Bob laughed. That funnybone hidden away in his makeup had responded. It was his first spontaneous laugh in a long time.

Chuck's older sister, Karen, listened to Bob playing songs

for the younger children and was touched. He appeared to be in a mellow mood and had played some light, happy songs. She told him she admired his dedication, but was not "where he was at" in her thinking. (Karen later joined the Peace Corps and spent two years in Africa.)

Rhea, my sister who lived in Houston, had not seen Bob since he left for COG some eight months before. I had not confided in her the true nature of the organization, and it puzzled her to see him so different.

"Bob keeps talking about the Bible, Frankie," she commented softly, "but I don't see any love in him or in what he's saying." She did not want to hurt, but she was honestly concerned.

For me the family reunion was a difficult time. One outgrowth of my competitive spirit had been inordinate pride in my children. I wanted them to look good before family and friends. It was a humbling experience to know that my family was viewing Bob's strangeness with pity. Humanly I was ashamed and embarrassed, and furious with myself for feeling that way.

"Letting go and letting God" doesn't come easy to the novice. Instead of being a shining example of new life, I was privately miserable, and it showed. I was not really trusting God to *do* anything, yet felt bound to keep my hands off. I spent much time running to our room to cry—and to try to pray. Putting faith into practice did not seem to be a simple matter.

Thanksgiving dinner, followed by the huge anniversary party on Saturday with hundreds of people attending, went by in a whirl. I have only a blurred recollection of what should have been a memorable occasion.

On Sunday evening Tom, Bob and I were left alone in the

mansion. Everyone else, having said their adieus, was traveling home. Kathy had flown back to school earlier, and we were
planning to start our trip back at dawn the next day.

The doorbell rang. It was Mary Lib and Hugh Neil, long-
time friends of ours. They had mistaken the date of the party,
and arrived one day late! After much laughter and chatter, we
invited them to stay for a cold supper with us.

Bob was upstairs and out of sight. Tom and I looked at each
other. We both felt this was the appointed time to have our talk
with Bob. We also saw, in some mysterious way, that Mary Lib
and Hugh were part of the plan. It was no accident that they
had arrived a day late.

Tom went upstairs to find Bob while I briefed the Neils on
the situation.

Tom reappeared with a reluctant Bob, placed our box of
evidence on the table, and started by telling our son that his
parents were active members of FREECOG. Then, in quiet,
measured tones, Tom began to reveal the facts we had discovered about the Children of God.

Mary Lib and Hugh had never heard of the group before.
They had each been brought up in fundamentalist, Bible-
centered churches, and become Episcopalians after marriage.
Now they attended St. John's Church, which had been my
original home church. Unknown to me, Mary Lib had just
finished a course on church heresies.

I have often thought since that evening of the wonder and
mystery of God's ways. Neither Tom nor I had realized it, but
we needed a moderator. Hugh, a brilliant physicist and the
founder and owner of a successful business in Knoxville,
revealed unexpected diplomatic abilities and slipped easily
into the role of facilitator.

He maintained an objective viewpoint the whole long evening, not speaking much, but seeing that we kept on track, supporting Bob when he made a good point, ensuring that each person had an opportunity to speak.

Mary Lib was able to point out with real authority why some doctrine was heresy; and she had the gift of being able to do so with humor and without putdown.

The Neils were just the balance we needed for that conversation. Furthermore, they both knew the Bible better than Tom or I did, and were able to correct with a light touch any errors in scriptural understanding that stemmed from the COG mentality, as quoted by Bob.

They did all this without once attacking him. In fact, they showed great love for Bob and tolerance for his position. They had not seen him for years, and Bob did not remember them at all, yet they had been given all the necessary empathy and wisdom for the occasion. (The Lord's emissaries are uniquely equipped, I have learned, even when they do not realize they are His tools.)

As the evening wound down, Mary Lib and Hugh sensed that their part was over, and left for home. Tom and I could see that Bob was far from ready to capitulate. In retrospect, it is clear that our expectations were unrealistic. No matter how we presented our FREECOG information, he was not prepared for an immediate about-face. I was disappointed, but not without hope.

Tom's reaction, on the other hand, was different—totally unexpected and out of character. When he had finished his presentation, which Bob rejected, Tom became livid with rage. I had never seen him so angry, and neither had Bob. It was scary.

After Tom stalked up the winding marble staircase, we could hear a couple of loud crashes above us; then all was silent. Bob and I looked at each other wordlessly. The huge, empty house seemed suddenly desolate and Tom's fury silenced us. We sat in the stillness awhile, immobilized.

I was not too surprised to hear Bob's next words as he stood up to leave the room.

"There's a COG colony here in Knoxville," he said flatly. "I'm going to leave right away and join them."

"All right," I said evenly, following him up the stairs. I didn't know what else might come out of my mouth. Then I heard myself saying, "But I want you to do two things before you leave."

He paused, turned slowly, and said coldly, "What two things?"

I was sending up a prayer dart as he paused. I didn't know what two things myself!

"One, I want you to read every piece of literature that we brought here about COG. You haven't had time to do that yet."

"And two?" he inquired, still cold. At least he had not said no.

"And two," I proceeded, once again opening my mouth in faith, my eyes traveling past Bob to the closed door of the master bedroom up ahead, "I want you to say goodbye to your father in person—not with a note, or by expecting me to tell him for you."

He turned away and began to walk slowly down the hall. Then he stopped, looked back and said, "O.K., Mom," in a normal, even kind voice.

I slipped into the master bedroom, closing the door softly behind me. Tom's breathing told me he was asleep.

I stood there a long time with my back against the door, letting the relief flow over me. I was remembering once again a crystal ball snow scene with the whirling snowflakes falling into place as peace descended.

Thank You, Lord, I prayed silently. *You put the right words into my mouth when I didn't know what to say. You sent Mary Lib and Hugh when we needed them.*

And I even felt that Tom's anger had assumed a rightful place in the evening and was perhaps an important part of the plan.

From somewhere deep inside me came joy and confidence. From such small things, I knew, faith grows. What was it the Bible said? "If ye have faith as a grain of mustard seed . . ." (Matthew 17:20). The tiniest of seeds!

Lord, You came through once more. You showed me in the most unexpected ways that You are indeed in charge, if I will only allow You to be. And trust You! And know that You are not going to do it the way I would. Letting go and letting God can be quite an adventure! Thank You, my Friend.

With a smile on my face, I fell into the best sleep I had had since Bob's return. On the face of it, things did not look good; yet when one has the audacity to claim "friendship" with the Almighty, miracles happen!

21

The Pharisee

Tom's diary entry about the episode that night in Knoxville reveals a little of what he was feeling:

> *Confrontation with Bob about evils in Children of God. I was very angry and very foolish.*

In fact, the next morning Tom was conscience-stricken. He was ashamed of his lack of control and felt he had really blown it.

I had become sure, on the other hand, that the honesty of his reaction, though explosive, had done more good than harm; and I tried to convince him of this. But a mental hangover held him in an iron grip.

At any rate, Bob climbed into the car with us, and neither he nor I mentioned his statement of the night before that he planned to leave us. We just acted as if we expected him to go with us.

The trip back was different. Everyone's true colors were flying. Although the air was thick at times, and Bob seemed stiff and unyielding, I felt it was healthier. I could give honest reactions, since we were no longer tiptoeing around on egg-shells. We asked questions about the colony and listened to Bob's responses with love and interest. When we did not agree, we said so, but without rancor.

I had brought along a book about Jesus' parables that I'd been studying. So I commented that the Children of God did not seem to mention the parables very often. Bob admitted this was true. He felt it was because COG focused instead on discipleship.

I felt it was because the parables were open to many levels of understanding and interpretation, which didn't fit in with the way the COG leadership operated. They wanted narrow, black-and-white explanations of the Scripture. In fact, they did not want any independent thinking among the Children.

But when I became bold enough to express some of these ideas, critical of COG doctrine, Bob just clammed up.

I spent a lot of time in silent prayer when Tom and Bob were talking. It helped me, anyway. I felt much more relaxed than I had since his return. I didn't want to analyze this new freedom; I just wanted to enjoy it. And I was relieved when Tom made no apology about his display of temper the night before. He, too, seemed more at ease. Maybe the "fireworks" had cleared the air.

In the motel that night I memorized I John 4:18: "There is no fear in love; but perfect love casteth out fear: because fear hath torment. He that feareth is not made perfect in love." It spoke to me in the still quiet hours when I could not sleep. And the following morning at breakfast, I shared with Bob those words and what that whole chapter about God's love meant to me.

I felt a sort of puzzlement in Bob about us. His parents were different from the ones he had left to join COG. But we didn't discuss ourselves. We talked instead about the Lord, and His love, and His Word. That's all Bob would respond to.

As we drew nearer to Houston, I could feel the tension returning. Bob began to seem more remote, less reachable. The stiff, cold manner and glassy eyes returned. I felt chilled when I glanced in the back seat at the "stranger."

The new Scripture helped, so I said it silently to myself, adding verse 16: "And we have known and believed the love that God hath to us. God is love; and he that dwelleth in love dwelleth in God, and God in him."

I could see Tom was tense, with his anxieties beginning to show. He made a few more persuasive attempts to reach his son, repeating some of his arguments of the night before, but Bob had turned us both off. He had already intimated that he had about two weeks total time at home and planned to go back by then. Maybe sooner.

We both felt that too much pressure now would precipitate an early departure on Bob's part. Yet we were through pussyfooting around. I remember shooting one last volley of words into the back seat before silence fell:

"One thing in particular breaks my heart, Bob," I said. "You have such a fine, inquiring mind—a mind capable of achieving so much. But in the Children of God you can't use it. You can't even go to a library. Even if you were determined to limit yourself entirely to Bible study, they allow only the King James Version. The King James is beautiful, but that requirement is a hindrance to learning all that God wants to say to you through His Word.

"If you wanted to study Greek to learn the deeper meaning of the words, and perhaps a truer translation, you couldn't do it. If you wanted to look into the first-century historical or political or social life—the pattern of life contemporary with Jesus' own time on earth—you couldn't do it.

"Oh, Bob," I cried out passionately, "you'll just stagnate there!" Tears brimmed my eyes as I glanced back to see his response.

"I do not want to live and work among you Pharisees," he snapped, and began a rambling discourse on the parable about the publican and the Pharisee.

All his COG mannerisms were in full display when, in complete exasperation, I turned, pointed my finger at him and shouted: "You are the Pharisee, Bob! Every time I look at you I see the Pharisee spirit!"

Up to that moment he had been a stone wall, with nothing I said penetrating. Now, for a fleeting moment, a look of pain crossed his face. I barely caught it. Then the mask was back in place.

After that final barrage, no one said a word. We drove the rest of the way home—some sixty miles or so—in strained silence.

After unloading the car and getting resettled, Tom sank into his favorite chair in the den, his face a gray mask. He looked completely dejected and defeated. Bob had gone to his room, and the house seemed as empty as if he had already left to go back into the Children of God.

My heart went out to my husband. He had been so confident that when Bob saw the damaging material that FREE-COG had collected, he would be as horrified as we were, and glad to leave the cult.

"We've lost, Frankie," said Tom, his voice almost a groan of pain.

I ached for him and with him. Tom's stability had been such a mainstay for me through the years. To see him crumple—even a little bit—was always devastating.

This time, however, I discovered I had a source of strength supporting me from somewhere else. My compassion for Tom gave me the empathy that enabled me to experience his hurt with him, yet I found my own pain was being offset with hope. I wished I could give it to Tom as a gift.

My wish was granted sooner than expected. Later that evening I was able to relay to Tom some encouraging news: Bob had gone over, of his own volition, to see Frances Ryan.

Color returned to Tom's face. I had been allowed to give my husband a small offering of hope. Faith could not be far behind.

I was just beginning to understand the meaning of a verse I had heard discussed at the Temple, and also in Janie's class: "Now faith is the substance of things hoped for, the evidence of things not seen" (Hebrews 11:1).

Could I have faith, even as Tom and I stayed home praying for him, that Bob was reconsidering?

22

Breakthrough

The next day Frances filled me in about Bob's visit with her. She had had to sit and listen for a long time to the Children of God teachings, especially about the end times. I asked her if she had been able to set Bob straight.

"To tell you the truth, Frankie, that did not seem to be my mission last night," she responded. "I could barely keep my mind on what he was saying. I just could not get interested. But . . . ."

She paused a moment. I waited.

Then she continued softly, "I just loved him, silently, from a distance."

It brought quick tears to my eyes. Since then, I have found that when someone says or does something that reveals to me the Lord's life in action, I am touched. The immediate response can be a king-sized lump in my throat or eyes unexpectedly brimming with tears.

Frances had patiently let Bob go on until he ran out of steam. Then, changing the subject, she offered him an inexpensive guitar she had—hesitantly, since she knew Bob was used to fine musical instruments.

"It was the first normal reaction I've seen in Bob since he returned," she commented. "He let his delight peep through for just a second. Then he started playing and singing some COG songs I did not like at all. They were bitter songs about persecution and what's wrong with the world."

Frances told me she had said to him, "You need to show forth His love. That's what really draws people to the Lord."

She didn't even think Bob heard her. But he had agreed to go with her to Newman's house—and that was encouraging.

The next day Frances drove up to the front of our house, tooted for Bob, and they were off to Newman's. I found myself on my knees in my "prayer closet"—the study—asking God for guidance and wisdom for Newman and Frances, asking Him to give Bob ears to hear, confessing my own fears, and asking Him to cast out those fears.

"Perfect love casts out fear," I reminded the Lord. "I want to believe again as I did that night that You are making Bob whole. You alone are perfect Love. You alone can eliminate my fears. You alone can make Bob well."

But as I prayed, I felt I was bargaining with God, or challenging Him somehow. It didn't seem right.

Then the phone rang. It was Frances. She had had to leave Newman's house to take her daughter to a dance class. She told Bob that she had to be gone awhile, and he barely nodded. We both thought it hopeful that he wanted to stay.

"But Bob is sitting on Newman's couch like a zombie," Frances continued. "I don't even think he's blinked. And, at least when I left, Newman hadn't even sat down. He was pacing the floor and talking forcefully."

Then she added, "He's anointed to speak to him, Frankie. It's a beautiful thing to see."

I didn't know what she meant, but it sounded encouraging. Then Frances went on to answer my unspoken question.

"Anointing in the Bible usually refers to placing oil on someone's head in a ceremonial way. It brought with it a special empowerment for service. Oil is also symbolic of the Holy Spirit. I believe Newman is anointed with the Holy Spirit to speak to your son, Frankie. He's speaking with authority, as from God. But even though he's talking powerfully, you can hear love and compassion in every word."

"What is he talking about?" I ventured timidly.

"Mostly he's talking to Bob like a Dutch uncle, letting him know he's blowing it by being associated with that group. But he's doing it all with Scripture, either quoting it or making reference to it. Newman knows the Bible as well as anyone I know."

"That sounds encouraging."

"Well, I can't see that it's having any effect on Bob yet. But it's bound to eventually, because Jesus' love is showing all through Newman's words."

Frances promised to keep me posted. And as the afternoon wore on, I felt my spirits lifting. I was able to shift my prayers from petition to praise.

Reflecting on Frances' explanation about the symbolism of oil, I reread the paper on "Disappointments?", remembering the reference to oil in there.

> This day I place in thy hand a pot of holy oil. Draw from it freely, My child, that all the circumstances arising along the pathway . . . may be anointed with this oil.

I had asked the Lord to teach me about what that meant on the day that my Greek "angel" first sent along this paper. Now

He was doing just that. How wonderful to know that I could draw on the Holy Spirit to anoint every circumstance! Yet it also meant I had to keep my eyes on the Lord.

Frances called again after dark. She had been in and out of Newman's house several times, having to leave to attend to her family's needs. Now that her children were fed and bedded down for the night, she was on her way back to Newman's.

Newman's own family, as it "happened," was away; and due to some other circumstances he was free to spend all this time with Bob. That had to be the Lord!

"Bob looks like a man of stone," Frances told me over the phone. "He's still got that weird look in his eyes, and I can't tell if he's receiving anything. But each time today that I've left, I've asked if he wanted to go, too; and each time he's shaken his head.

"It's amazing, Frankie, but a few times when Newman stopped to rest, I had a Scripture or a thought that meshed exactly with what Newman had been saying. I felt it was the Lord."

I *knew* it was the Lord.

"What about food?" I asked.

"Believe me, no one is thinking about eating!"

Since Tom was home by now, he talked with Frances briefly, thanking her for her concern and all that she and Newman were doing. Then she was gone again.

The hours crept by.

What happened next at Newman's house I did not learn about for months. But I want to describe it now, in the context of when it happened.

The pattern never varied all evening. Newman spoke with persuasion and eloquence, words from the Bible, words of truth. They were the only words that could register with Bob, saturated as he was with the Children of God's emphasis on Scripture. Frances filled in from time to time when Newman stopped to rest or pray silently.

Bob barely moved a muscle. His expression never changed. He was free to leave at any time, yet he never seemed to want to go.

It was two o'clock in the morning when Newman finally stopped. Frances knew he had finished. Neither one of them had any more words to say. Silence descended.

Bob sat there in his lonely place, mute and apart from them, separated by his lack of response.

Newman left the room, while Frances and Bob continued to sit in silence. In a few moments Newman reappeared. He had a towel on one arm and a bucket of water in the other hand. Kneeling in front of Bob, he slowly removed Bob's shoes and socks.

Then, looking up into Bob's face, he asked softly, "May I?"

Now the stillness in the room was even more penetrating than before. After a pause, Bob gave his assent with an almost imperceptible nod.

Newman performed the humble rite of footwashing with care and tenderness, following the example set by Jesus on the night before His crucifixion. It is an act that requires dual participation—that of servant, and that of willing recipient. Bob was no longer in isolation. Contact had been made.

Gently the servant washed the dirt of the road off the feet of the wandering one—one whose seeking had caused him to travel a dusty road indeed.

Frances was deeply moved. Then she saw something that touched her even more.

A single tear was making its way down each of Bob's cheeks.

23

Yoyo Days

If there had been a breakthrough, Bob was not yet ready to acknowledge it. Frances and Newman, having been obedient to God's leading in that marathon session, continued now in their faithfulness by staying out of the picture. They believed the next move was Bob's.

Tom had several business trips out of town around that time, which threw Bob and me together a lot. Bob spent most of his time alone in his room in Bible study and prayer. I was doing the same thing. At least he was making no move to leave.

Through several quiet phone conferences with FREECOG members, I learned that many Children who had come home for Thanksgiving had already returned. Most had been contacted at least once by phone before disappearing silently back to their colonies.

I knew it could happen to us, too. But, strangely, the phone did not ring for Bob. No COG contact at all—at least, not to my knowledge. (I couldn't be there all the time.) No one in FREECOG had any surefire solutions, though there were many suggestions. The only advice I heeded came from Rose Marie and Charlsie. It was: "Keep your eyes on the Lord."

One day a FREECOG mother who knew Bob slightly appeared unexpectedly at our front door to chat with me. She had not realized Bob was home. When I told her, she asked if she could talk with him.

My first instinct was to put her off. The balance was so delicate, and I knew she was bitter and frustrated by her own son's involvement. But the only direction I seemed to be getting from my prayer sessions was to trust God in the circumstances. This circumstance, as I saw it, was that the mother was here and wanted to see Bob; and my part was to trust God in this situation.

I remember feeling shaky as I went to get Bob.

She spoke to him frankly about the pain and anguish their family was experiencing because of the Children of God. Then, right before she left, she put her hands on his shoulders and spoke directly to him, unabashed at the tears running down her cheeks; and she begged him to stay home.

I wasn't sure, but it seemed to me he was touched, though he said nothing to give me a real clue.

At least now he had seen a parent's distress firsthand. We had not shown him ours—not openly, anyhow—afraid that anything that seemed to play on his sympathy could boomerang. Maybe he needed to see it through someone else's trauma; and if I had blocked it from happening, a vital link in my son's rehabilitation would have been eliminated.

God's message through the prophet Isaiah was so clear: "My thoughts are not your thoughts, neither are your ways my ways, saith the Lord" (Isaiah 55:8).

The next time the circumstances seemed wrong to me, I was a little bolder to trust God in them, even though the next event appeared riskier than the one with the FREECOG mother.

It began on a very "down" morning when Bob seemed on the brink of returning to the COG. I had left the house to escape the tension, plus the fear of saying something that might tip the scales the wrong way; and I'd driven to a nearby Christian bookstore.

Jeff, the young manager, had come to know our story when, soon after Bob's entrance into the cult, I had marched into his shop, furious and frustrated, and asked for a book to refute the Scriptures Bob was quoting us.

Although I didn't realize it at the time, Jeff began on that first day to minister to me and put the Lord's love around me. About the same age as my son, he seemed to have a wisdom beyond his years. He had steered me gently to the Bible as the Book I really needed to study. He had helped me understand the messages in it long before Bob came home. To me, his shop was always an oasis of peace.

This particular morning, Jeff's advice after hearing about the mother who had wept over Bob was simply this: "Continue to trust God in the circumstances."

When I got home, I found Bob listening with rapt attention to the proselytizing of two young men who had "the answer" for him. They represented another group professing to be Christians, but their "something else" was their own translation of the Bible, which denied the divinity of Jesus Christ.

From what I had been able to put together, they believed Christ was a spirit creature—the archangel Michael, who was created by God and became the Messiah at His baptism, a god but not God.

One look at Bob, with those strange staring eyes back in place, made my heart sink.

He'll be off with them next, I thought.

I left the three of them and fled to my bedroom, falling in despair onto my knees.

"You sure make it tough for me!" I exclaimed. "Was this really necessary? How on earth can *they* help the situation?"

I was furious.

Trust Me.

"I'm angry. I don't want to be angry. But this is too much!"

Trust Me.

"I know Your ways are higher than my ways. And You tell me not to lean on my own understanding. But—"

Trust Me.

I remembered the bigness of Him and the smallness of me. It seemed ridiculous to argue.

"I'm trying to trust You," I said. "Help me."

Slowly peace came.

Bob did not want to discuss these new contacts, but I saw him reading their literature over the next few days, apparently fascinated by it. I wanted to warn him about it and speak out against this new danger, but I felt a restraint. My part was to trust, not to try to solve everything myself.

For the old, self-sufficient me, this new role was not easy. It kept me on my knees a lot.

Rose Marie came by one afternoon to visit. We had a fire in the den and Bob joined us as we talked. The coziness of the fire, combined with the warmth of Rose Marie's personality and her ease of manner, enabled the three of us to hold a near-natural conversation.

We talked about a number of things before it turned to the Children of God. Then, in an ordinary voice, Rose Marie began to discuss the sexual misbehavior of the leaders, which she knew about for a fact.

I wanted to change the subject, afraid that Bob would become defensive and belligerent, as he had in Tennessee when we had given him similar facts. Instead, I saw shock in his eyes. He questioned her at length. She was calm, matter-of-fact and very convincing.

I knew that Bob, a product of his generation, was no prude. But he needed to believe in the integrity of those in charge who called themselves Christian leaders. And I felt that her words shook him.

As Rose Marie left that day, she handed me a book to read. It was about cults; and though it said nothing about the Children of God (since they were too recent to have made the roster), it included a full chapter on the sect to which the two young men belonged.

I read that chapter in particular and left the book on the hall table with no comment. (I hoped that was not overstepping the bounds of just trusting. After all, I was leaving it up to God to put the desire in Bob to read it.)

And He did. Bob took it to his room one evening. Then he had two more long sessions with the same two young men, on different days that week. Each time I disappeared to my room to pray. Then, after their last meeting, I found Bob in the den, burning all their literature in the fireplace.

"What happened?" I asked, taken by surprise.

"Mom, do you remember that first day they came? You had gone off in a huff that morning, and I was ready to take off for Dallas."

I nodded.

"Well, after you left, I really prayed. I told God I could see that you and Dad thought I was confused. I didn't believe I was, but I asked Him to show me in some way if I really was mixed up. I also asked Him to send someone of His choosing to guide me. In only a few minutes, the doorbell rang and it was those two guys.

"I knew God had sent them. That's why I read everything they gave me so carefully, and really listened to them. Then, when your friend left that book, I felt I should also read that. Today I was sure of the message."

He stopped. My heart began to beat fast with hope, but I didn't want to seem too eager.

"Mom, the Lord showed me through them that I *am* confused about some things. I could see that those guys are, too. He also showed me how they've taken the Scriptures and twisted them. You and Dad have been saying that the Children of God do that, but I thought you were wrong. Now I can see how it might be possible. I'm not ready to say COG has done that—just that it's possible." His voice trailed off.

"Oh, Bob!" I cried, and he let me hug him before he disappeared once again into his lair.

Like an animal licking his wounds, I thought, he needed solitude and time to heal. It enabled me to leave him alone when my instinct was to pursue this advantage without letup.

Secluded in my room, I continued my ongoing conversation with the Lord. This time I was full of awe and admiration. Praise came naturally.

"I hope I'll never question Your methods anymore," I said. "Who but You would have thought of that! And if I had succeeded in my thing and gotten rid of those young men, or argued with Bob about them, I could have thwarted Your beautiful lesson."

It was an "up" day for sure! I felt the scales had been tipped our way, and that we had won. Surely it was over.

The next days were downers, though. Bob was cold and uncommunicative. As if he had gone too far in saying so much, now he shut himself off from Tom and me and came out only in his Stranger guise. When I tried to get him to talk about his admitted confusion, he would have none of it.

Bob began to make sounds about going back once more. He

took to going out for long walks, or riding one of the girls' old bikes he found in the garage. I was never sure when I heard him leave that he would come back.

Sometimes then I would hop into my car and drive over to Jeff's shop for encouragement. Frances and Newman also kept in touch by phone and lent prayer support. They were still waiting for Bob to come to them.

And so the "yoyo" days went—up and down, up and down. Tom, being away so much, did not feel the tension as I did, but he and Bob had some good talks. Then I found myself wishing he would just tell Bob to quit all this foolishness. If only he would lay down the law!

Then I'd come to my senses and realize that Tom was doing naturally what I was struggling to learn how to do. He was trusting God in the circumstances to turn his son in the direction we knew to be right.

I would often hear Bob working on music in his room. Usually it had a COG ring to it, which made my heart sink. Although the two weeks were up, and I knew I should be grateful he had not gone back yet, I was afraid he was leaning toward returning—especially when he played such downbeat music.

One day the music sounded peppy and contagious. I noticed my foot keeping time automatically with the beat. It drew me to his room, and I knocked on the door.

"What's that? It sounds so happy," I said, coming in and perching on the foot of his bed. I felt friendly and sensed his response.

Bob seemed pleased and relaxed; the magic of music had done its work. I could not have chosen a better time to approach him, and I had not planned it at all!

"Well," he said with a touch of shyness, "the Lord has given me the music for one of the psalms. Here, follow it in the King James."

It was from Psalm 124. He began to fill the room with notes of pure joy. Frances' twenty-five-dollar guitar took wings, and so did my spirit.

"If it had not been the Lord who was on our side," he sang, "now may Israel say; If it had not been the Lord who was on our side . . . ."

The song was lively and free and I loved it. I didn't pay much attention to the words, excited by the glow I saw in him.

But as he sang out, this line caught my ear:

"We are escaped from the snare of the fowler; the snare is broken and we are escaped!"

The words sounded strong and clear. Suddenly I knew what he was thinking. He envisioned this as a battle song for his brothers in COG. He still saw the world, the establishment, this materialistic society, as a trap set by Satan, the fowler. But through the Children of God, they had escaped the snare and were "free," like birds.

My soaring spirit plunged earthward like a kite plummeting to the ground. I slipped out of the room, offering a small goodbye smile to hide threatening tears. I needed time alone to assimilate the shock of this quick revelation.

"O dear God, let him see what the real snare is," I prayed when back in my room. "He's looking at those words from one side, and I'm seeing them from another! If he still thinks of this world and our life as the trap, we are helpless to help him. Please open his eyes once and for all to the real danger. Show him that the enticing lure of escapism through the cult world is, for him, the real snare of the fowler."

My sense of helplessness increased by the moment, and my dependence on God grew apace. I could hear the winding down of Bob's song as he sang the closing words, getting softer and softer. They found their way through the crack under my door and curled around me like a fog blanket. But they ended up comforting me:

Our help is in the name of the Lord,
Who made heaven and earth.
Blessed be the Lord,
Blessed be the Lord,
Blessed be the Lord!

24

Escaped from the Snare

The next day was my birthday. Bob had been home 25 days. I felt as if I had been living on the edge of a precipice, and I was tired. It came as no big surprise that morning when he hinted once more that he was going back.

"I'm learning to trust the Lord for my direction," I told him. "I believe you are, too. If that's what He's saying to you, then you should do it, and your father and I will have to accept it. It still doesn't seem to us that that is His will for you, but each of us has to hear Him for ourselves. Maybe, if you're taking a step this momentous, you should discuss what you're hearing with a spiritual elder like Newman or Frances."

Bob shrugged.

With that I left to go to Janie's Bible class, feeling suddenly emancipated.

They prayed for Bob and me that day. I was given a sureness that it was all in God's hands in a way I hadn't felt before. I was trusting Him, whether Bob went back or stayed home, and that was new!

Bob was still there when I returned home, but I made no more effort to discuss it with him. Tom soon arrived with a beautifully wrapped birthday present for me—a large leather-bound King James Bible. On the flyleaf he had written:

Presented to Frankie, by Tom, on the occasion of her first birthday in a new life. December 17, 1971.

I was delighted, especially touched by his inscription. Then I noticed another little note with unfamiliar handwriting attached.

"What's this?" I asked, holding it up.

"Oh, that's from Lynne Argyries, your little Greek angel. You know I cannot wrap presents. She did the wrapping for me, and sent along a note."

Feeling the need to meet this girl who kept figuring into my life, I called and invited her over for dinner the next evening. Tom had mentioned a boyfriend, so I suggested she bring him along too, if she liked.

They arrived in midafternoon, an enchanting pair. Tom made the introductions. Lynne, a vibrant, slender wisp of a girl with a glorious halo of dark curly hair and enormous, soulful brown eyes, hugged me in the most natural, unaffected way, and made an instant hit with me. John was a tall, gentle giant with a kind, sweet manner. I thought him handsome with his reddish-brown hair and full, neatly trimmed beard. Both appeared to be in their twenties.

Bob was home, but secluded himself in his room when he heard that someone from Tom's office was to be there. We left him alone.

It was a dark, dreary day, and we spent the afternoon getting acquainted before the cheery fire in the den. Lynne was eager to hear the details of Bob's return, having heard only the bare facts from Tom. Then they told us about the evangelistic efforts of their church.

Once I suggested getting Bob, but Lynne stopped me.

"Frankie"—she used my first name with ease—"John and I both know the Lord has called us here to witness to Bob today. So we don't have to arrange anything. He'll do it. Just relax and let it happen."

I was amazed. I had never heard anyone talk like that, except maybe Frances. There was boldness in Lynne's manner, yet it was not offensive. It simply reflected a sureness in her foundation. She knew where she stood.

Later on she asked John if she could share with us something about them. He smiled and nodded his head, his eyes twinkling, as though she were a wayward child and he the indulgent father.

"John and I were to be engaged," she confided, "but the Lord just did not give me any peace about it. I don't know why. I finally had to tell John, and he's been so good about it. So now we're just friends. In fact, our relationship is better than ever."

John, a graduate engineer with a fine Houston firm, seemed to me an excellent prospect for any young girl.

Lynne helped me in the kitchen as it neared time to eat. I missed my girls, and really enjoyed her company. Still no sign of Bob. About fifteen minutes before dinner, Lynne called to John. He came and looked at her solemnly.

"I believe it's time for you to go get Bob," she said.

He nodded his head wisely.

My amazement grew. They *did* know what they were about! I pointed the way to Bob's room and John disappeared.

I was suddenly struck by a ludicrous thought. Since I figured Bob had probably fallen asleep in his room on this dark day, and since John looked just like all the pictures of Jesus painted through the ages, I began to imagine Bob's shock at being awakened by the Lord Himself. I could hardly keep my hilarity under control. I wondered if this was an example of the Lord's humor.

John was back quickly and announced that Bob would be along soon. I lit candles on the dinette table and the four of us sat down together. Bob appeared, looking stiff and austere and very out-of-it. Tom said the blessing, then asked Lynne how she happened to come to Houston from New York.

I had been secretly deciding not to say a word during the whole meal, and was relieved to hear Lynne launch into her story. In a quiet, rich voice, with bright wit and a light touch, she gave her history. Sensing an importance in the occasion, I scarcely wanted to breathe.

When Lynne finished her tale, no one said anything for a moment. Bob had on his Stranger face, cold and unbending. I noticed he had watched her intently with no expression while she spoke. Now she leaned forward slightly, looking at him.

"Are you depressed?" she asked with astonishing directness, her face the picture of honest concern.

There was not a sound in the room. Now I *couldn't* breathe! Tom looked stunned.

"Yes, I am," answered Bob, a little defiantly.

She leaned forward even more, gracefully putting her hand out on the table toward him as if to touch him, and spoke in the kindest, most loving voice. They seemed to be alone. The rest of us were shadows.

"Tell me all about it," she said gently.

There was a timelessness about the moment. No one moved. I have no idea how long we hung there.

At last Bob spoke. His face had relaxed perceptibly. And when he grinned, he looked almost like Kathy's brother again. I wished Kathy were there to see him.

"You're in for quite a tale," he began, and she nodded encouragingly.

With that, as we ate, he began to tell her the story of his life. He talked and talked, pouring it all out. Details we had never heard and views we had only suspected were mixed in with facts we already knew. The hurt, the confusion, the seeking, his music, his need for it. The story of his coming to the Lord, and how he had joined the Children of God, and how he was now in torment trying to decide whether or not to return.

Tom and I glanced at each other in wonder as we finished our meal and the precious moments moved along. The floodgates had been unlocked. All that had been pent-up now came rushing out.

Up until then, many had been sent to speak to Bob: uncles, aunts, cousins and grandparents at the golden anniversary, not to mention his own sisters and brothers-in-law, and Mary Lib and Hugh arriving by "mistake." Then there was Frances, Newman, Rose Marie and the other FREECOG mother; the two young men who rang the doorbell, as if on cue; and his own father and mother. There were probably others I did not know about. And there was a reason for each of them.

Then came these two, one to wake him from physical sleep and the other to wake him from mental bondage. I felt Bob had been called forth from the dead. Now there was just the matter of unwinding the graveclothes.

"Would you play some of your music for me?" Lynne asked, her voice hushed. She was beautiful, her eyes luminous in the flickering candlelight. Her classic Greek features seemed to be aglow. How could he refuse?

As he went to get his borrowed guitar, I raised my eyebrows inquiringly to Tom. Was this the time to give him our Christmas gift?

He nodded, and I went to get our hidden present for Bob. We had bought him a fine, secondhand guitar with a rich, mellow tone. He had told us not to get him anything for

Christmas, but we had heard of this special instrument and gotten it anyway, just in case he stayed home.

When he returned, I handed it to him in its case, un-wrapped, and made a little speech:

"Bob, even scholars are not sure of the exact date Christ was born. Therefore, your father and I have selected this moment to present our gift to you for Christmas. But it has one 'string' attached."

I looked to Tom for support, since we had agreed upon this earlier. Tom nodded for me to continue.

"This guitar is for your ministry 'in the world.' If you decide to go back to the Children of God, it isn't yours to take to them. It's only for your use here. This was your father's re-quirement, although I agree."

He wavered for a minute. I thought he might refuse it. Then he reached out for it without a word. He opened the case and took the guitar lovingly into his hands. When he strummed it, it was in perfect tune. (This, I found out later, was something of a miracle! It had been two weeks in my closet, and we didn't know when it had been tuned before that.)

Bob came quickly to me and kissed me. Then he went to the other end of the table to embrace Tom. Everyone was teary.

Back in his place once more, Bob began to play and sing with joy and verve. It was a precious, never-to-be-forgotten time. We watched the graveclothes being unwound. Another miracle was happening before our eyes.

John had a deep, pleasant voice, and he joined in on some of the familiar choruses. Lynne just sat there looking like an angel. Bob sang on and on, all Christian songs. When Tom requested his favorite, "What Is Love?" (Bob's simple piece that Tom had also requested at Mingus), Bob explained pa-tiently that he did not plan to sing secular songs ever again.

"Sing it once more for your father, please," Lynne asked.

"I'd like to hear it, too. And I've often found that just by changing a word or two in worldly songs, they can be effective in a coffeehouse ministry. Sing it, and I'll show you what I mean."

She is either the cleverest girl I have ever seen, I thought, *or else she is truly being led by the Lord. She knows just what to say and when to say it.*

What is love?
It's something very real.
It's a joy in your heart
That you just can't conceal.

Our son began to sing, his eyes on the lovely apparition across the table from him.

"It's beautiful," said Lynne when he had finished. "There's not anything that needs to be changed." There was honest admiration in her voice. "If you wanted to give it a more Christian flavor, you could do just a slight rewording." She paused a moment. "The third line could say, 'It's *God's* joy in your heart.'" Then she sang it with him.

The Lord had been saving a special treat for the last: Lynne had a beautiful trained voice, which blended perfectly with Bob's! They became one voice. I could see the surprise in Bob's face as she sang with him.

The music and sharing went on for awhile longer. At one point, while we were singing a rousing chorus, I saw Bob throw back his head with eyes shut, lift one arm heavenward, hold up his new guitar with the other and sing, "I'm free, I'm free!"

He was free indeed! The realization streaked across my thoughts like a skyrocket on the Fourth of July. He had escaped. Yes, escaped!—from the snare of the fowler.

The next morning while Tom was shaving and I was putting on my makeup, he said, "Honey, do you think—? Bob and Lynne . . . . Do you suppose—?"

It was not like him to falter that way.

"Don't say it, Tom," I broke in. "Don't even think it. She's so wise and mature. And he's still not healed. And then there's John. But—" Now *I* was stumbling.

We looked at each other and laughed. We were on the same wavelength. And the Lord seemed to be doing one miracle after another around here. Nothing could surprise us anymore!

> For eye has not seen, nor ear heard, neither has it entered into the heart of man, the things which God has prepared for those who love him.
>
> (I Corinthians 2:9, author's paraphrase)

Tom's diary holds this understatement:

Lynne A. and John with us for dinner to talk with Bob. She's something.

25

The Chief Physician

From that day on, Bob began to show signs of recovery. It was not an instantaneous healing. The snare had effectively pinned his wings, crippled him mentally and emotionally, taken the light out of his eyes, and blinded him in many areas.

There was much to overcome: confusions that weighted him down and bitter shame at having been trapped. He needed to restore and rebuild many relationships.

Now my eyes were opened to the ways of the Lord that flowed naturally through our circumstances, revealing His order, His perfect use of time and space (when we allowed it), and reflecting His love and concern for all His children, with special tenderness for the lost and hurting. I found myself greeting each new day expectantly, eager to see God's working out of all the details of our son's recovery.

Here are a few of my observations:

I saw the youth pastor at the Evangelistic Temple, Buddy Hicks, stretch out a hand of love and welcome to Bob while he was still tainted with the Pharisee spirit of judgmental self-righteousness.

Buddy knew Bob's story from Frances and Newman. He

invited Bob to join their youth team on their annual Christmas ski trip. This merry group of young people, alive with the Lord's love, blanket the hills of a Colorado ski resort every Yuletide in a witness for Jesus Christ.

Buddy made him feel like an important member of the team, and the trip was instrumental in helping Bob make the transition from the cult world to this world. It was a risky step for Buddy, since he did it at a time when many of the COG attitudes were still very evident in Bob. Yet he could do it because he trusted the Lord to redeem any mistakes, and because he knew it would hasten Bob's recovery.

Buddy also allowed Bob to sing at the "Youth Quake" (Friday night youth meeting at the Temple) with music of his own choosing, again trusting the Lord to guide Bob in his selection. Bob took to bouncing the songs off Frances first, and she would show him why some of them were not right. He could take it from her.

Right before Christmas, Bob received the first phone call from COG since he left them. (We have never discovered why they did not contact him sooner, as they did others who came home.)

A girl involved in the music ministry, whom he admired, was their bait. It was a long talk, but he refused to bite. He told her he was considering staying home; that he needed more time.

Then, while he was off with the "ski witness" team, they called again. I confess to a certain impish pleasure in being able to reply truthfully, "Oh, Bob's gone on a ski trip with some Christian friends."

They never called again.

Meanwhile, I was allowed to see how deeply ingrained some of the COG teachings had become.

Once I mentioned to Bob that, because of things being revealed about the erratic behavior of Moses David Berg, I wouldn't be surprised to see him being eased out of headship by other leaders.

Bob gave me that cold, blank look and said with the old COG inflection, "I don't see how that is possible. Moses David is the end-time Prophet!"

I was too startled to reply. Yet once this remark was out of Bob's mouth, I could see his own realization of the fallacy he had expressed. It was like a poison hidden within him that needed to be spat out to help bring him to good health.

Once, Bob made a confession to us that must have given him relief the way the lancing of a boil would. He described some of the indoctrination he and others were given by the COG before they left on the holiday exodus.

They had been briefed thoroughly on how to "spoil Egypt." We, his parents and family, represented Egypt. Those COG members going home for the holiday were to get every material item they possibly could from "Egypt" to bring back to their colony.

The Scripture reference for this was Exodus 3:22: "But every woman shall borrow of her neighbor, and of her that sojourneth in her house, jewels of silver, and jewels of gold, and raiment: and ye shall put them upon your sons, and upon your daughters; and ye shall spoil the Egyptians."

Bob said he never intended to do that himself, and I don't believe he could have. He had even implored us not to give him a Christmas present, at a time when he still expected to go back. Nevertheless, he had listened to the teaching of this policy, did not refute it when it was taught, and never told us about it until he had decided to stay home.

I have since learned that such an "elitist" perspective—one that says, "We are the special ones; we have the right to certain things because of our special relationship with God"—is one of the hallmarks of a cult.

FREECOG invited a specialist to come to one of our meetings to guide us in relating to those of our children who came out of the Children of God, ostensibly to visit, but intending to return. He was an ordained pastor as well as a psychologist.

Although Bob had already decided not to go back, I attended this meeting and made a list of the pastor's suggestions.

To my amazement, I was able to write below each one how the greatest Psychologist of them all had arranged neatly for the working out of every suggestion. It was already done!—and so much more thoroughly than we ever could have accomplished in our own strength.

1. When he comes home, arrange for your child to be with those who loved him in the past, peers especially, to discuss things.

God's solution: The golden anniversary at which those who knew and loved Bob best were gathered. There were 19 first cousins present, many in his immediate age group. They all loved him, and showed it, but listened and let him talk. Then, in blunt but kind words, they voiced their nonacceptance of COG.

2. Arrange to spend a lot of uninterrupted time with your child to "listen and love," and again, to talk things out.

God's solution: Four days "trapped" in the car to and from Tennessee. Other days alone with parents at home later.

3. Arrange for a trained psychologist or one trained in moderating skills to assist in a serious airing of differences.

God's solution: Mary Lib and Hugh Neil, as already

described, but trained and prepared by One who knew what skills were needed for the moment.

4. Since you're dealing with hostilities on both sides, there's need for honesty and forthrightness in actions as well as words. Don't be afraid to show honest emotions, such as anger or true distress. This should be kept within bounds, however, and not be constant anger or distress.

God's solution: In particular, Tom's startling anger explosion, because of its honesty (revealing how much he cared) and its rarity.

5. Arrange, if possible, for someone your child admired and respected in the past to be available to talk to him frankly, with love, when he is prepared to listen.

God's solution: Frances, backed by Newman. No man's method, no matter how well-planned, could possibly match that divinely inspired time with its words of truth and love spoken in a language dear to the heart of our son, and with the footwashing as an *Amen*.

6. Arrange, if possible, for your child to be with peers he did not know before, but who are well-rounded, stable examples of his age group. This is not so much to challenge as to get him to open up.

God's solution: Lynne and John. Need more be said?

All of this was evidence to me of our Father's all-seeing, all-knowing wisdom, and His deftness in handling each need so easily yet so naturally, with the means at hand, through people He sent—some aware of their mission and some not.

I saw also how easy it would have been for me, with my penchant for wanting to run things, to have spoiled the working out of His plan. In fact, I had come perilously close any number of times to doing just that.

How exciting to contemplate that at key points I had been one of the instruments used by the Master Planner! I could see more clearly than ever the importance of being in close rela-tiontionship with Him; of seeking His guidance; of listening for and being aware of Him in all circumstances; and of draw-ing freely from the pot of holy oil.

I saw our son gradually beginning to draw from that holy oil himself. New music began to emerge that reflected his re-covering relationship with the Source of all beauty. Also, Bob was prayerfully seeking God's guidance and confirmation that he was where he should be.

A friend of mine from church, hearing that Bob was home, stopped by one day and asked if he would lead her class in song. Margie Blossman has been teaching Sunday school for fifty years. An elfin-like child of God, she is a delight to all who know her.

Bob, taken off-guard by her sprightly charm, accepted. (He had never been asked to do anything at our church before.) Later he found, to his surprise, that she taught the four-year-olds. He had expected teenagers and had no idea what to sing to tots, except maybe "Jesus Loves Me."

I came home one afternoon that week to find Bob sitting crosslegged in the backyard, his guitar on his knees.

"Look here," he said, holding out his hand.

In his palm were several different kinds of seeds, ranging in size from a minute speck, which was responsible for a per-sistent weed in our lawn, to a large pinecone, which had dropped from one of our trees.

"I've been marveling at all these sources of life right here within my reach," he said, "and the Lord gave me this little ditty."

He began to pluck his guitar and sing in various ways a simple little song containing these lines:

> Oh, the seed that you sow
> Is the seed that will grow.
> If love is what you sow
> Then love is what will grow.

It was catchy, and I began to sing it with him, my heart dancing at the miracle of what God was doing in him. When I remarked what a perfect song it would be for Margie's class, his eyes widened in surprise. This had not occurred to him.

That Sunday he returned from her class full of awe. When he had arrived, Margie had been busy at the windowsill, her back to him. She turned, saw him, smiled and said: "We're going to plant seeds in our window box today, children. Bob, do you know a song about seeds?"

It was just the confirmation he had been looking for!

Bob composed other music, joyful and triumphant, that warmed us. Many melodies fitted together so well that he often sang them as a kind of medley, a hymn of joyful praise from the heart of one bursting out of the prison of confusion.

One day I told Bob I wanted him to meet a young friend of mine who ran a bookstore.

"Jeff?" he asked, startled.

"You know him?" I exclaimed.

It turned out that he did. Bob had bought a cross from Jeff before he left for the Children of God. After his return, lonely and seeking fellowship, he took the old bike from the garage one day and rode over to the bookstore to renew the acquaintance. Jeff had been in the unique position of ministering to both mother and son, and had never said a word to give it away, bless him.

Bob and I drove over together to tell Jeff that the secret was out. The three of us had a delicious laugh about it. Jeff confided that he had learned a lot about the Lord's timing through the experience. It seems that Bob would often arrive on the heels of my departure, and vice-versa. Jeff felt sure we would stumble over each other one day, but we never did.

I might have been a lot more relaxed during that time of tension if I had realized that Jeff, so loving and wise and full of the Lord, was counseling Bob. But evidently it was not part of God's plan. Maybe I would have become dependent on Jeff rather than on Him.

There was another surprise awaiting us, too: one day while signing a check for a book I was purchasing, we discovered we shared not only the same unusual family name, but the same great-grandparents as well!

Jeff and I turned out to be second cousins, and he and Bob second cousins once-removed.

"Just think, Jeff—the Lord has known about this ever since we met," I said as we danced around the store in excitement, no other customers present.

"Frankie," Jeff replied, stopping his merry jig and looking at me solemnly, "He's known about it since the foundation of the world."

And of course He has. The chance of our meeting and discovering our similar roots in a city the size of Houston must have been astronomical!

"I always knew you were my sister in the Lord," said my newfound cousin. "But I never dreamed you were kissin' kin"—and he leaned down to kiss me.

"I wonder what I did for excitement before I knew the Lord," I laughed.

And exciting it truly has been. And joyful, and full of adventure, too, from that day to this, ten years later.

Did Bob become whole?

Of course he did! His recovery was in the hands of the Chief Physician, the One who truly heals. All remnants of the fowler's snare have been blown away by the wind of His Spirit. I would never have written this book without Bob's knowledge and full permission. He has encouraged me all along the way.

What happened to Lynne, my little Greek angel? She and Bob began to sing and minister together for youth groups, in coffeehouses and in churches, showing His love to the world.

Eleven months after they met, Bob and Lynne became truly one in the Lord. They were married by Buddy Hicks in the chapel at the Evangelistic Temple. The gathered body, most of whom had seen the miracle evolve, worshiped the Lord together in thanksgiving and praise. It was an all-out celebration, giving glory to God who had made this union possible.

In one touching, unforgettable moment, the bride and groom sang a song to each other before they said their vows. It contained these words:

> Must be the Lord I hear
> In the garden, among the trees.
> Here we are in Eden,
> Just we three.
> We are in love, you know,
> The Lord, myself and thee.

Later Bob told me that he had learned the song while in the Children of God. To me it was an appropriate touch. I saw it as symbolic of the creativity of the God of love, who brings beauty out of ashes and turns our mourning into dancing.

Epilogue

He that dwelleth in the secret place of the Most High shall abide under the shadow of the Almighty. I will say of the Lord, He is my refuge and my fortress: my God; in him will I trust. Surely he shall deliver thee from the snare of the fowler . . . .
(Psalm 91:1-3a)

Our soul is escaped as a bird out of the snare of the fowlers: the snare is broken, and we are escaped.
(Psalm 124:7)

Those verses sum it up. The words now penetrate my outer shell of consciousness and invade my inner self as a soothing balm. Our son was delivered from the snare of the fowler. The words are more than a promise. They are an actuality. God is who He says He is. God does what He says He will do. He is trustworthy.

Yes, He is faithful, indeed!

In recent years the Children of God have centered their activities in Europe. *Time* magazine stated that COG has "evolved into a brigade of international nomads, embracing the religion proclaimed in hundreds of 'Mo' letters. . . . They not only advocate the 'playboy' philosophy, but the ancient practice of religious prostitution."

From the testimonies of ex-members, it appears that "Mo" is also into spiritism, and claims to have a "spirit-medium guide."

According to a recent article by Louis Moore, religion editor of the Houston *Chronicle*, one of Moses David's letters, containing a distinct messianic ring, proclaimed Libyan strongman Khadafy as hero and world leader. "The relationship between Khadafy and the Children of God," wrote Mr. Moore, ". . .in the light of current events, seems both fascinating and frightening."

Satan has done his work well with this group.

With most of the COG colonies gone from America, FREE-COG is no longer active. How grateful I am, however, for the supportive role this group played in our situation! Another helpful organization in uncovering cult activities has been Spiritual Counterfeits (P.O. Box 2116, Berkeley, CA 94702.)

Here is one thought-provoking statement from the Spiritual Counterfeits Project Newsletter (September 1976):

> It will do very little good for the church to confront cults unless we simultaneously confront our own participation in the conditions which have produced them. The ultimate spiritual counterfeit is a Christianity which has all its distinguishing authenticity squeezed out of it, a Christianity which is culturally co-opted, socially irrelevant, doctrinally correct and spiritually dead.

The answer for us Christians is to be so knowledgeable about the foundations of our faith, the truth of the gospel and the reality of Jesus Christ that we can immediately spot something phony, doctrinally unsound or even heretical, that tries to call itself Christian.

Walter Martin, in his book *Kingdom of the Cults,* gives a good example of how one segment of the business world goes about detecting counterfeits.

He states that the American Banking Association sends hundreds of bank tellers each year to Washington, D.C., in order to teach them how to spot counterfeit money. They do this by not allowing the tellers to touch or see anything but the original during the entire two-week training program.

The reason for this, according to Walter Martin, is that the American Banking Association is convinced that if a man is thoroughly familiar with the original, he will not be deceived by the counterfeit bill, no matter how like the original it is.

Paul speaks to us today through his words to Timothy as he warns him not to be naive about false doctrines, and to be ready to guard the truth with love:

> The Lord's servant must not be quarrelsome but kindly to everyone, an apt teacher, forbearing, correcting his opponents with gentleness. God may perhaps grant that they will repent and come to know the truth, and they may escape from the snare of the devil, after being captured by him to do his will.
>
> (II Timothy 2:24-26, RSV)

I became aware of the fowler and his snares through my exposure to the cult world. But I have come to see that cults are only one example of a snare. As a nominal Christian, I, too, had been ensnared. Anything that diverts us from the fullness of the life so freely offered to each of us should be called "the snare of the fowler."

There is no doubt that each of our family members has been affected profoundly by Bob's cult experience. Once, reflecting on Romans 8:28, Bob remarked that he didn't believe it was God's perfect will for him to have been in the Children of God; yet he could still see various ways God had used it for good within his family as well as in himself.

First Becki, our eldest, the pragmatic intellectual, came home to see "what on earth has happened to Mother," and found the reality of new life in both her parents, as well as a "lost" brother not only found but healed!

She and her husband, Max Bishop, were so affected that they, in turn, committed their lives to Christ in a new way. In 1975 they moved from the suburbs into the heart of Detroit, to become part of the Episcopal Church of the Messiah and its mission to the inner city.

Though Max has a job he loves with a computer firm, his faith is also a full-time occupation. Becki has a new peace as she explores fresh ways to use her talents within the community. Their three young daughters attend the school that the church operates for the neighborhood, and they are flourishing.

Our second daughter, Susan, impressed with Bob's deliverance, also made a new commitment to the Lord. She and her husband, Andy Klemmt, and their young son all had their lives changed drastically when Susan developed a rare, serious muscle disease that continues to be the focus of many prayers. We are grateful for the expert medical care she is receiving, and are trusting God for her healing. Susan's faith is staunch, and Andy has proven to be a man with a marvelous blend of diverse qualities, including strength, tenderness and humor.

Kathy, our youngest, had a difficult time following her baptism in the Holy Spirit at age 16. Back in school, her tender little green shoots of faith began to wilt, or were trampled. A period of rebellion followed, but she belonged to the Lord, she knew it, and she returned to Him with strengthened faith.

As she matured into a glowing young woman, she evolved from "Kathy" into "Katherine"—which suits her. She began to attend a Bible-centered church, where she met and later married a handsome Purdue graduate, Michael Enyart. They have two daughters.

During the wedding ceremony, Bob and Lynne sang four beautiful songs. Three of them were anthems Bob had written, but the fourth was Paul Stookey's "Wedding Song," confirming Katherine's prediction of seven years before that her brother would sing that song at her wedding.

As for Bob and Lynne, Tom and I watched from the sidelines with bated breath as their initial attraction progressed, waned for awhile, then blossomed into real love.

When they first began to date, it seemed that the Lord in His wisdom brought Lynne to some pitfalls in her walk of faith. She had appeared mature and unattainable on the night they met. But as she stumbled a bit and her vulnerability was exposed, Bob was able to minister to her in a way that helped to establish a better foundation for marriage. Her strength helped pull him out of the snare, and his faith muscles were invigorated as he aided her in her trials.

Following their marriage, Bob and Lynne attended Evangelistic Temple in Houston and became part of a youth ministry that traveled to Europe at the request of Teen Challenge International, to help set up Teen Challenge centers in Paris and Amsterdam.

Today they live in Houston and are music leaders together at Church in the City, a unique fellowship of Christians with a vision of ministry to the inner city. Their congregation features a number of "house churches" that meet during the week in different neighborhoods scattered over this vast metropolis, then come together on Sunday for joint worship.

Recently Church in the City produced *The Worship Album* (Star Song Records, distributed by The Word Company, Waco, Tex.). Though recorded in a studio with an orchestra, the music is typical of a Sunday morning worship service in their church. It includes four of Bob's songs, and features him as soloist in most of the music. Lynne's lovely voice blends with him on several of the hymns and lends a sparkling vitality to the finale, a round with a fugue-like quality.

Bob and Lynne have three little daughters now, and many of Bob's songs reflect his love of his family. Another focus of his gift for music has been to make Scripture come alive in song. The two of them sing at weddings and other occasions around the area, their purpose always being "to show forth His love."

Tom and I had our eyes opened to the availability and reality of God through this whole experience. It came with lightning-bolt quality for me; while Tom, in his own words, was "oozed" into a new understanding. To discover that a personal relationship with the Almighty is possible is a breakthrough, but to explore that relationship daily is heady adventure.

Our own relationship as husband and wife has deepened and matured in the exploration. Praying together and seeking God's guidance for our lives comes naturally now. In fact, it's a joyful necessity! In the process we have been set free to walk through that which has been prepared for us (from Ephesians 2:10), trusting the faithfulness of the One who calls us, and who also will do it! (See I Thessalonians 5:24).

Our new life focus has involved us in such things as "Faith Alive" and "Cursillo," two renewal movements active in the Episcopal Church; in teaching adult classes in our parish; in

Tom's development of a powerful "listening ministry"; and also in the creation of this book.

We have found that sharing the gift of new life with others is no heavy responsibility. Instead, due to the bubbling, effervescent, irresistible qualities of the gift itself, we are actually energized as we allow it to flow naturally.

We have also come to see that the Christian life was never intended to be pale, anemic and powerless, but a celebration, glowing with the hope of a vivid rainbow—sparkling, triumphant, victorious!

Scripture tells us that "all thy children shall be taught of the Lord; and great shall be the peace of thy children" (Isaiah 54:13). The lessons come in many forms. In our case, a snare of the fowler was used for our instruction.

To the truth of Isaiah's words, each member of our family can say only, "Amen!"